RHONDA K. HOLLAND

ISBN: 978-1-940682-42-6

Contents

Shut the Door

Introduction

Shut The Door! Three little words jumped off the pages at me as I looked again to a very familiar and loved passage of Scripture found in 2 Kings 4. Two very different women with two very different stories are found in this chapter in the Word. I have heard these stories countless times over the years and have loved hearing them preached and taught. But I had never noticed those words, "shut the door," until this time in my study. Why now? What was it that the Lord wanted me to see? As I prayed for direction, it began to unfold in my heart.

Both these women, while their stories and circumstances were different, were in many ways actually in the same situation. They both desperately needed a miracle. They both sought and were dependent on God's guidance They both fervently loved their children. They both were in a crisis that neither of them created. And they both looked to God and found exactly what they needed, *after they shut the door!*

In this study, we will take a look at these stories. My prayer is that we will understand from the Word of God exactly what we need to do to shut the door to the enemy and his influence in our lives. We will read about these two very different women with very difficult problems—but their answer was the same! God delivered them both as they <u>shut the door</u> to the circumstances they were faced with, and instead deliberately set out to hear from God. They then walked in obedience to the leading of the Spirit of God, and the results for both were beyond their hopes and dreams. *God's plans always exceed our dreams!*

I am so thankful that we can follow the examples given in the Word and experience the same sufficient power of the Holy Spirit today.

The Word of God is eternal. It is timeless—forever unchanging. Yet His forever Word is always a fresh Word for us. His timeless Word is always a timely Word when applied to our circumstances. It is the Living Bread that continually guides, comforts, and strengthens us.

As I write this study, my sincere heart's prayer is that you will find the courage to go forward with full anticipation of God's delivering power accomplishing in you and through you what He has promised. We will <u>shut the door</u> to the enemy's plot against God's plan for our lives. As a result, we will experience renewed hope of God opening doors for us that nothing and no one can shut.

> *I know your works. See, I have set before you an open door, and no one can shut it; for you have a little strength, have kept My word, and have not denied My name (Rev. 3:8).*

WEEK ONE

Proper Perspective

Guarding the Oil in My House
2 Kings 4:1-7

There are two very interesting stories about two women and God's miraculous intervention in their situations recorded in 2 Kings 4. While these women came from totally different walks in life, they had one important thing in common: they both served and loved God. And they each witnessed God perform the impossible when they shut the door to the outside influences and focused on their faith. It is vital to note that it was their focus on God and making His presence a priority in their lives and homes that caused them to have proper perspective, even in the face of their most difficult trials.

This proper perspective enabled them to shut the door to the enemy's plan of destruction. Proper perspective will do the same for us!

In the first week of our study, we look at the recently widowed mother and her situation as it is written for us in 2 Kings 4:1-7. We read about the woman who was the widow of one of the sons of the prophets who had studied under Elisha's teaching. This poor widow was the mother of two sons. She was left with no money and debt she couldn't pay. The story opens with her crying out to Elisha in desperation for help. She didn't waste any time voicing her problems! She knew Elisha and she discerned correctly that he was a man of God. Her discernment required action. She was deliberate in her choice to reach out to the man of God. And she got right to the point—*she made her petition known.*

> *A certain woman of the wives of the sons of the prophets cried out to Elisha, saying, "Your servant my husband is dead, and you know that your servant feared the Lord. And the creditor is coming to take my two sons to be his slaves," (v. 1).*

Interestingly, Elisha addressed her plea with two questions. She then answered with a statement that she felt would express adequately her dilemma.

> *So Elisha said to her, "What shall I do for you? Tell me, what do you have in the house?" And she said, "Your maidservant has nothing in the house but a jar of oil," (v. 2).*

I can only imagine her helplessness. She was probably embarrassed to express her lack, but her desperation overcame her shame. She had nothing left in the house but a jar of oil. Historians have written that she had likely sold everything she owned. All the furnishings, food, clothing, and other essentials were not named when Elisha asked what she had remaining. This indicates everything had been sold except the one remaining item—a jar of oil.

I had always read this account from a different perspective than I have now. Before when reading this story, I felt as if she was saying, *I have nothing but that little bit of oil and what good is that to me.* In the light of her circumstances, it certainly seemed inadequate for her needs and those of her sons. But I see it completely differently now.

The Jewish historian Josephus wrote that this needy mother was the widow of the prophet Obadiah. Many theologians agree. So, perhaps this oil was anointing oil and the only sentimental item she had remaining of her life and ministry with Obadiah. Women are certainly sentimental—I know I am! Perhaps this jar of oil held memories she regarded highly. One could only wonder and with my imagination, I certainly have. Regardless, I believe she kept it for a purpose, on purpose. She had sold all she had except this jar of oil. There was nothing else left in her house. We know from the account given later in this passage that the oil itself was a marketable commodity. But even in her desperation, for some reason, she had kept this particular jar of oil.

POINT TO PONDER:

In the Word of God, we understand that oil often represents the Holy Spirit and His anointing. It also signifies the presence of the Holy Spirit. It is crucial that we realize the power of the Spirit of God in us. Proper perspective of the presence and power of God in our lives will cause us to change our focus. We won't look at what is wrong and what we are lacking. As followers of Jesus Christ, we will look at Whose we are and what He can do in the midst of our crisis. We will remember the importance of keeping oil in the house (the Holy Spirit) at all costs. If there is oil in the house, all things are possible.

So, oil in the house will cause you to have proper perspective, and proper perspective will cause you to keep oil in the house!

✳Let's take a moment and look at a familiar parable and consider its meaning:

> *Then the kingdom of heaven shall be likened to ten virgins who took their lamps and went to meet the bridegroom. Five of them were foolish (thoughtless, without forethought) and five were wise (sensible, intelligent, and prudent). For when the foolish took their lamps, they did not take any [extra] oil with them; But the wise took flasks of oil along with them [also] with their lamps. While the bridegroom lingered and was slow in coming, they all began nodding their heads, and they fell asleep. But at midnight there was a shout, Behold, the bridegroom! Go out to meet him! Then all those virgins got up and put their own lamps in order. And the foolish said to the wise, Give us some of your oil, for our lamps are going out. But the wise replied, There will not be enough for us and for you; go instead to the dealers and buy for yourselves. But while they were going away to buy, the bridegroom came, and those who were prepared went in with him to the marriage feast; and the door was shut. Later the other virgins also came and said, Lord, Lord, open [the door] to us! But He replied, I solemnly declare to you, I do not know you [I am not acquainted with you]. Watch therefore [give strict attention and be cautious and active], for you know neither the day nor the hour when the Son of Man will come (Matt. 25:1-13 AMP).*

There is much to be said and learned from this parable. Without oil in their lamps, there was no light, no direction, no illumination. Without light, there is no clarity—no revelation. Destruction always hides in darkness. When we walk in darkness, it is impossible to have proper perspective. We can't walk in the path God has for our lives without His light, and we certainly can't lead others in truth when we are in darkness. Instead of shutting the door to the enemy and his influence, we instead open the door to his plot. So, the enemy wants more than anything to steal your oil. He would love for you to sell or trade it for something the world has to offer.

The lack of oil (the Holy Spirit) will also cause our light to go out and will render us powerless to the plot that awaits us in the darkness of Satan's snare. We must be like the wise virgins illustrated in this parable. We must keep oil in our lamps at all times. Remember, all ten of these virgins in the parable started out with oil. But five of them—*half of them*—became careless. They were distracted and complacent. They lost their proper perspective. They had an oil leak and didn't even realize it until it was too late.

> *Is there oil in your house? And are you guarding it carefully?*
> *There are possessions we can let go of that in time*
> *will cost us nothing of eternal value.*
> *But we must never lose the oil in the house!*

Let's read the next two verses in the passage in 2 Kings:

> *Then he said, "Go, borrow vessels from everywhere, from all your neighbors—empty vessels; do not gather just a few. And when you have come in, you shall shut the door behind you and your sons; then pour it into all those vessels, and set aside the full ones," (vv. 3-4).*

Elisha immediately instructed her to take a proactive role in her own miracle. He told her to go and borrow vessels from all of her neighbors—lots of empty vessels. He further instructed her to bring those empty vessels home then shut the door and pour.

He didn't explain to her how this miraculous filling of the vessels would happen and there's no indication that she asked. *But I know she wondered!* Yet still, she maintained her perspective. She was determined to <u>see with faith</u>. She looked beyond her circumstances, and instead, by faith, she looked with confidence to what God was about to do. How do we know this? Because she did as instructed without question. She sent her sons to borrow empty vessels.

> *If my focus is my problem and where I am in the midst of it all, then where I am is where I will likely stay. I must instead focus on where I am going and, by faith and obedience, I will get there. The circumstances I am facing are temporary. I must look beyond the moment. Proper perspective in the battle is crucial.*

Let's take a few moments and read this familiar passage of Jesus' words in the gospel of Matthew.

> *"Therefore I say to you, do not worry about your life, what you will eat or what you will drink; nor about your body, what you will put on. Is not life more than food and the body more than clothing? Look at the birds of the air, for they neither sow nor reap nor gather into barns; yet your heavenly Father feeds them. Are you not of more value than they? Which of you by worrying can add one cubit to his stature? "So why do you worry about clothing? Consider the lilies of the field, how they grow: they neither toil nor spin; and yet I say to you that even Solomon in all his glory was not arrayed like one of these. Now if God so clothes the grass of the field, which today is, and tomorrow is thrown into the oven, will He not much more clothe you, O you of little faith? "Therefore do not worry, saying, 'What shall we eat?' or 'What shall we drink?'*

or 'What shall we wear?' For after all these things the Gentiles seek. For your heavenly Father knows that you need all these things. But seek first the kingdom of God and His righteousness, and all these things shall be added to you (Matt 6:25-33).

What is it about this passage that brings you comfort when you are faced with uncertainty in your life?

_____

_____

_____

_____

_____

_____

_____

When you are faced with a crisis, what passage of Scripture do you often turn to that helps you have proper perspective?

_____

_____

_____

_____

_____

_____

_____

_____

Meditate and pray these verses in your prayer and devotion time this week. Journal about them and commit them to memory. They will help you have proper perspective when faced with life's battles. Remember, the enemy cannot defeat you when the Word of God is your weapon of choice.

Now, let's go back to our story of the widow and her sons. After she came back with her sons, they were to enter the house with the borrowed, empty vessels and <u>shut the door</u> and pour. Why was it imperative that she bring her sons in and <u>shut the door</u> behind them? It was of great importance that her sons witness and participate in this miracle. *Their witnessing this supernatural multiplication of the oil would forever change their perspective.*

POINT TO PONDER:

The world is filled with borrowed and emptied vessels. We will discuss this more in this lesson, but it is important that in our focus to bring in the lost and weary of the world, that we not forget our own. Our sons and daughters must also feel and know that they are significant and important to us. We must include them in our work for the Kingdom of God. So often in ministry, if we are not careful, we can become so focused on the lost and hurting, we lose sight of those dear and near to us. It is important to note that she came back with her sons as instructed. Our family is so significant. They are our first priority and those we influence the most. Let's make sure we keep them close and help <u>shut the door</u> of the enemy's plan for their lives. As we continually gain proper perspective through the Holy Spirit's guidance, that same insight will also become theirs.

Our children need more than just our account of what God has done. Though our testimonies are of great influence and worth, our children also need to witness firsthand and experience for themselves the power of God at work in their lives.

I also find it interesting and worth pointing out that Elisha's presence wasn't necessary for this miracle to become a reality in the widow's home. The miracle required two things:

oil and obedience. The presence of the Holy Spirit and obedience—these are the same requirements for us today for God to move in our situations. When we obey, there is always faith at work. Obedience itself is a testimony of one's faith in God. It clearly reveals that you are persuaded God is up to something—even though you may not know exactly what it is.

So, not only was she to bring in her sons and the borrowed and empty vessels, she was to *shut the door* behind them. I believe this was to shut out the negative comments and doubts of others. Elisha knew she needed to close out all distractions and negative outside influences and focus on her faith in God. She was to embrace her sons in faith, not fully understanding what God was going to do next, but trusting He was up to something. As a result, she and her sons would be witnesses to the filling of borrowed and emptied vessels.

In the natural way of thinking, it certainly would have made more sense to have heard, *Go borrow flour or bread. While you're borrowing, ask if they can give a donation to help cover the debt.* She could imagine Elisha using a plan like that and those borrowed items to create something to help her out of an impossible situation. She could imagine someone else having what it would take to produce a miracle. What she had seemed so insignificant. But no! She couldn't go borrow other people's supplies. She was to go borrow a lot of containers to carry the one thing she felt she already had—emptiness! God was going to demonstrate His ability to take a little bit of oil, her obedience, and a whole lot of emptiness and turn it into a miracle.

We have all had times where we felt empty and hopeless, in need of direction and answers. But remember, the anointing of the Holy Spirit—the oil in your house—can stop the plot of the enemy and give you direction that takes you to your victory. Greater is He that is in you than he that is in the world!

Take a moment and write a prayer of thanksgiving for God's faithfulness and His assured presence in your battle.

_____

_____

_____

_____

_____

_____

The enemy wants you to focus on the emptiness and lack but God wants you to focus on His powerful presence and the possibilities that come as a result.

Imagine with me for a moment what it must have been like for those neighbors Elisha referenced. This widow and her two sons were going door to door borrowing empty vessels when all they seemed to have in their lives already was emptiness. Their plight no doubt was being talked about in their community. Everyone was wondering what this widowed woman, with her world crumbling around her, was going to do next. But this—this never crossed their minds. Borrowing vessels—*empty* vessels! Why? Everyone's curiosity must have been awakened. They were likely discussing it among themselves.

> *But remember, we are not borrowed. We are bought with a price.*

She and her sons felt like borrowed, empty vessels. Everything familiar was gone. In the eyes of the world, they had nothing worth anything. They no longer felt like they belonged to themselves. This mother's heart was breaking. Her sons—her posterity, her joy in the present and hope of the future, all that really mattered to her—were soon to be the property of the creditors. These young sons would be borrowed away from their true purpose and destiny if something didn't change quickly. And now, these soon-to-be-borrowed and already-feeling-emptied vessels were told to go borrow empty vessels. Yes, everyone must have wondered why—including themselves. *How would these borrowed, empty vessels be filled by empty vessels?* But even in their feeling of emptiness, they went against their own struggles and walked in obedience. And God fought the battle for them.

> ***They were soon to be reminded that they still had what really mattered after all—they had <u>oil in the house!</u>***

Have you ever felt borrowed and emptied? Have you ever felt pulled from every direction by every situation and circumstance around you? Often in life, in raising our children—even in ministry—that can become the normal way of living rather than the exception. But remember, we are not borrowed. We are bought with a price.

> *You were bought with a price [purchased with a preciousness and paid for, made His own]. So then, honor God and bring glory to Him in your body (1 Cor. 6:20 AMP).*

> *You were bought with a price [purchased with a preciousness and paid for by Christ]; then do not yield yourselves up to become [in your own estimation] slaves to men [but consider yourselves slaves to Christ] (1 Cor. 7:23 AMP).*

POINT TO PONDER:

Have you experienced well-doing weariness? Often when we are feeling weary in doing what others consider ministry, are we, in fact, yielding to the plans of man instead of God? Are we being borrowed away from the One Who purchased us and His perfect plan for our lives? Are we becoming enslaved to man's agenda as we are warned in 1 Corinthians 7:23, rather than God's? If this describes you, be careful because the borrowed feeling often proceeds the emptiness. Emptiness is the feeling that comes from no oil in the house.

Have you ever felt like you were running on empty? How did this happen? How have you ministered to others but now feel emptied and drained yourself of the presence of God in your own life? How do you feel void of the Spirit of God working in you? In week two of our study, we will address oil leaks in our houses. Often we lose oil when we are borrowed out and not walking according to God's plan for our lives.

As you pray and journal this week, seek God sincerely concerning your agenda. Have you taken on tasks He didn't ask you to take? Have you lost proper perspective in all of your going and doing? <u>Are you guarding the oil?</u> We all have responsibilities that are part of life. We are to provide for and take care of our families. But are you running to and fro, trying to please others at the expense of your family and the ministry God has entrusted to your care? Are you feeling weary and borrowed instead of joyful and fulfilled in your calling? If so, perhaps you have been borrowed away from His plan for your life. Seek the Lord sincerely for direction. He will lead you and you will find that place of refreshing again in Him.

✳

When we are doing the will of God, He strengthens and renews us by His presence and power. He assures us that when we walk with Him, His yoke is easy and His burden is light.

For My yoke is wholesome (useful, good — not harsh, hard, sharp, or pressing, but comfortable, gracious, and pleasant), and My burden is light and easy to be borne (Matt. 11:30 AMP).

I confess that I have read this passage in numerous translations trying to grasp its truth. I read it again and again in one of my seasons of emptiness, wanting it to mean something else! I didn't want to come to terms with the fact that I had built for myself crosses God never intended for me to carry. I had put more on my plate than God had required—sometimes with a little help from others. But because I was doing good I felt I was walking in obedience when in truth, I was walking out of step with Him. Some of the things on my agenda were actually taking time away from what I was really supposed to be doing. I couldn't understand why I was often experiencing anything but an easy and light burden. It was only when I came to the realization that I could and should lay down some of the things I felt I was to carry—things that God had never intended for me to pick up—that I was set free of the emptiness and weariness that comes from being borrowed away from His purpose for my life.

He will come through for us again in every situation.

The widow woman didn't go asking to borrow money or food or send her sons to do so. She had no way in sight of paying that back. But she could borrow vessels filled with emptiness. That would prove to be an easy task. After all, no one minds giving away nothing! But God had plans to do something amazing with the emptiness she borrowed and that she felt she already possessed. Her obedience to Elisha's instruction without questioning his command was trust—it was <u>faith in action.</u> And that obedience would soon turn her own nothingness and emptiness, as well as that she had borrowed, into something incredible.

Yes, it's likely the neighbors were talking among themselves, and some would've questioned them as to why they asked to borrow empty vessels. Some may have scoffed or mocked them, *Don't you have something more productive you can do? Don't you realize the serious situation you're in?* Fear could have taken hold and stopped them from their assignment as they pondered the facts facing them. If they had listened to the naysayers that may have questioned their actions, they likely would have stopped short of gathering enough vessels, if any at all. But they were undaunted in their mission to gather empty vessels as Elisha instructed. When they got home, they did as directed by him and <u>shut the door to everyone's opinion and doubt.</u> And their <u>obedience produced a miracle!</u> God would show them that He could take empty vessels and fill them to overflowing because of their obedience and *because there was <u>oil in the house.</u>*

> *So she went from him and shut the door behind her and her sons, who brought the vessels to her; and she poured it out. Now it came to pass, when the vessels were full, that she said to her son, "Bring me another vessel." And he said to her, "There is not another vessel." So the oil ceased. Then she came and told the man of God. And he said, "Go, sell the oil and pay your debt; and you and your sons live on the rest," (2 Kings 4:5-7).*

Isn't it wonderful that God is always more than enough. She was able to go and sell the oil and pay her debt and she and her sons would live on the rest.

Yes, we must guard the oil in our home. Spiritually, the Holy Spirit's presence will do the same for us. He will sustain us and bring us through. And when the battle rages again, we can reflect and remember His provision in past battles and live with full assurance that He will come through for us again in every situation.

They shut the door and God performed a miracle. Now, you must do the same!

Shut the door to the lies of the enemy and the negative opinions of others that contradict the Word of God. Remember that you are God's child and you have purpose in Him. Do not lose proper perspective. He will never leave you or forsake you. There is oil in your house. You may have suffered loss along this journey, but you still have your anointing and purpose. God's presence is with you and you will make it through.

The widow saw the borrowed and empty vessels all around her. But she also witnessed the miracle of them all being filled. I believe the Lord wanted her to see and understand that she and her sons could have been like those borrowed and empty vessels. *But because there was oil in the house, everything changed.*

The enemy will tell you that you will never accomplish your goals. But God's Spirit is with you.

Shut the door with:

> *I can do all things through Christ who strengthens me (Phil. 4:13).*

He will try and make you feel powerless against his schemes. *Shut the door!*

> *You are of God, little children, and have overcome them, because He who is in you is greater than he who*

is in the world (1 John 4:4).

Satan will whisper that your family and loved ones will never be saved. Declare this truth and *shut the door!*

> *But as for me and my house, we will serve the Lord (Josh. 24:15b).*

Doubt will plague you over your financial stress. *Shut the door* with the promise of His provision!

> *And my God shall supply all your need according to His riches in glory by Christ Jesus (Phil. 4:19).*

> *Look at the birds of the air, for they neither sow nor reap nor gather into barns; yet your heavenly Father feeds them. Are you not of much more value than they? (Matt. 6:26)*

Guarding the oil will cause you to change your perspective. You will see with the eyes of faith.

Look differently at your situation. If you are in a battle, I pray that you will not focus on what you don't have in the natural, but rather focus on what you do have through His Spirit. Don't focus on where you are in the conflict, rather focus on where you are going by faith in Him. There is oil in your house! Remember what powerful things God can do with His presence working in you. Don't be distracted by what others may think or by the doubts that have bombarded your mind.

Expect the emptiness to be filled.
Anticipate the need to be met when you shut the door.

POINT TO PONDER: *Important!*

Every Sunday, churches congregate together for worship. Just like the widow woman in this passage was told to go and borrow empty vessels and bring them to her house, we are to invite and encourage borrowed and emptied vessels to come to His house. How imperative it is for the church to maintain <u>oil in the house</u> so that these borrowed and emptied vessels can be filled. In this hectic and busy world we live in, so often we bring programs and entertainment to our churches to attract the crowds. The method used to attract the crowds may be different from church to church, but the need of the borrowed and emptied vessels is the same everywhere. They need the healing oil of the Holy Spirit to be poured and to fill their empty vessels. They hunger to be made aware that they have been bought with a price, and that void and emptiness can be replaced by the sweet Holy Spirit.

If the church hides the oil and replaces it with an appealing message or watered down theology for fear of losing the ones who come in, then we begin to take on the identity of the borrowed and emptied. We become nothing more than a social gathering place. Without the pouring of the oil, the world influences and changes the church rather than the church influencing and changing the world.

Read this powerful passage in Zechariah, a word given to Zerubbabel, that is so relevant to us today:

> *Then he said to me, This [addition of the bowl to the candlestick, causing it to yield a ceaseless supply of oil from the olive trees] is the word of the Lord to Zerubbabel, saying, Not by might, nor by power, but*

> *by My Spirit [of Whom the oil is a symbol], says the*
> *Lord of hosts (Zech. 4:6 AMP).*

We must keep and guard the oil in the house—both where we live and where we congregate. For nothing we do separate from Him will last. The Holy Spirit must be welcome in our homes and our churches. His presence must be honored and cherished. Then the borrowed and empty vessels will be filled and in turn will bring in other borrowed and empty vessels for that same infilling.

As you pray and journal this week, meditate on and memorize verses of Scripture that help you maintain proper perspective when you are faced with battles in this life. Proper perspective is necessary in helping you shut the door to the enemy.

Remember: Oil in the house will cause you to have proper perspective, and proper perspective will cause you to keep oil in the house!

I Believe / you say

WEEK TWO

Prioritize Please!

How to Avoid an Oil Leak

Psalm 139:23 & 24

Have you ever had an oil leak in your vehicle? I'm not talking about just the need to change the oil in your car; I am talking about a leak. There is a big difference. There are warning lights that appear informing you that you need to take care of the situation before it becomes a really major problem. Cars don't do well without oil! Trust me. I know all too well.

> *My words reflect whether or not there is sufficient oil in my house.*

I will never forget driving one hot summer day in Georgia years ago when it sounded like everything in my car engine exploded and hit the ground. My car came to a screeching halt. I wish I could say it wasn't my fault. But I had been so busy with my schedule and other pressing things that I hadn't been paying attention to a light that I thought was telling me I needed an oil change. Oh, I did intend to change the oil and take care of it—at a more convenient time. But I was so distracted by other things that I completely misread the warning light. The light was in fact trying to help me understand I needed oil. There was a leak. That car died that day and is very likely still in a junk yard somewhere in Georgia.

In last week's lesson we discussed the importance of guarding the oil in your house. We were reminded that the oil represents the Holy Spirit in the Scripture. The widow in 2 Kings 4:1-7 realized the value of preserving and keeping what really mattered. She sold everything else she had—but she kept the oil. God turned that oil and her obedience into a more-than-enough miracle in her life and home.

In this hectic, busy, over-scheduled, often stressful world in which we live, we must prioritize the things that are most important. We must keep first things first. The main thing must be the main thing in our lives.

Let's look again at one of the verses we discussed last week:

> *But seek (aim at and strive after) first of all His kingdom and His righteousness (His way of doing and being right), and then all these things taken together will be given you besides (Matt. 6:33 AMP).*

I like the way the Amplified Version brings clarity to this passage. We are to aim and strive after *first of all* His kingdom and His righteousness—His way of doing and being right. Then all the other things of importance will fall in their proper place. It will be easy for us to shut the door to the strategy of the enemy when God is truly first in our

> ### We must guard the oil at all costs.

hearts. He will lead us and we will in turn lead others by example. Our family, friends, neighbors, co-workers, and even our enemies will see we put God first and they will also witness God's faithfulness in action in our lives as a result.

So, how do we know when things are getting out of order in our lives? How do we recognize when we are starting to get out of balance? When do we first know that there is an oil leak in our hearts and homes?

Maybe we can better answer these questions by looking at a list of characteristics that are displayed in us when we *are* keeping the main thing the main thing—when we are prioritizing properly.

First of all, when I am keeping things in proper order, His *presence is always a priority*. I want Him to feel welcome in my heart, my decisions, and in my home. I seek His Word and His direction in my choices and welcome the Holy Spirit as my guide.

Also, my words reflect whether or not there is sufficient oil in my house. If I have a *positive proclamation* and speak the truth—His Word—over my situations and do not declare my circumstances as triumphant in my battles, then that is a sure indication that my priorities are in proper order and I'm guarding the oil levels. I often say, "Speak the truth and not the facts!" The facts say one thing but His truth (the Word of God) always trumps the facts.

My *pursuit of God is proactive* when my priorities are in order. I look forward to His presence. I enjoy church services and congregating with people of faith. I find that faithfulness in church attendance comes naturally and I actually desire to be in His house. I also pursue the Lord's presence in my prayer life and devotional times in His Word.

When my oil is full, my prayer life is enhanced. My *petitions are passionate* when I pray. When He is in His proper place on the throne of my heart, I can pray in confidence that He is hearing and answering my plea and receiving my requests. And I pray as He leads!

My *praise is powerful* because it comes from a heart that is focused on the awesome and faithful God we serve. When my oil is full, my cup runs over in gratitude. My praise reflects my heart's view of God. When the Holy Spirit is resident in my heart, my praise is an active and ongoing response to His presence.

Finally, when my oil is full, *His perfect peace*—peace that passes understanding—is mine, even in the midst of the trials. Like you, I have experienced this in my own life. I have walked in battles that were fierce, but when my focus was the Peace Speaker and not the storm, the Shepherd and not the valley, my heart was calm even in the raging winds of the struggles around me. Regardless of the battle you are in—whether spiritual, physical, emotional, or financial—when God is your focus, peace is the result.

Let's look at this oil level indicator list. When there is sufficient oil in my house—when the oil light is NOT blinking indicating a leak—I will have *proper perspective* and:

I will make God's presence priority in my home and heart.
I will make my proclamation positive
based on His Word and promises.
I will make my pursuit proactive and will not be
passive about God's guidance in my life.
I will make my petition passionate
and I will pray as the Holy Spirit leads.
I will make my praise powerful because
my God is worthy and my heart is grateful.
And I will experience His perfect peace in the process of it all.

So then, if these statements are indicative of a healthy oil level, we must assume that the opposite indicates a leak. Is the oil light flashing in your heart? Is there a leak that needs attention? Are you losing your focus on what really matters? Have you lost proper perspective?

Is God's presence priority? Or are you finding yourself less concerned about God's presence and more consumed with your schedule? Are personal devotions in the privacy of your home and with your family becoming more of an interruption to your routine rather than a part of it? Is God's presence in your home no longer a matter of importance, something you put off because you are pressed with so many demanding things to do? Do you feel you are simply too busy to read the Word or meditate on it?

Is your proclamation positive? Or are your words reflecting your doubts rather than your faith in God? I repeat often a statement I heard an evangelist say years ago, "If it's in the well, it's coming up in the bucket." Your words will come forth and are a sure indicator of what's going on in your heart. Are you finding yourself speaking more often negative and doubtful comments about circumstances you are facing, rather than declaring God's Word over them?

Is your pursuit proactive for God? Or is your pursuit of God less than it has been in the past? Have you lost some of your zeal and enthusiasm to be in His presence? Has attending church services regularly just become one more thing to do, and has it actually become an option with you? Do you find yourself spending more time entertaining yourself with things of the world rather than pursuing God? Are you seeking the advice of others more often than consulting Him concerning your choices?

Is your petition passionate when you pray? Or have you found yourself less driven to intercede? Are your words becoming hollow and repetitious rather than passionate when you do pray? Has your time in prayer been reduced to moments? And are those moments no longer consistent?

Is your praise powerful for all His benefits and blessings? Or have you lost your desire to worship and praise God for His faithfulness and His daily blessings in your life? Have you lost your gratitude? Are you focusing more on what is missing rather than on what you have been already blessed with and promised?

✱ *Have you lost your peace and find yourself stressed in the midst of your battles?* Are you more quickly irritated and often depressed and discouraged? Are you feeling hopeless instead of hopeful? Are you fearful and apprehensive? Are you provoked to anger easily?

We must take the time in this study to do some honest self-evaluation. If you can see yourself developing a negative pattern in any of these areas, then there is an oil leak and you are on your way to becoming a borrowed and emptied vessel—borrowed away from your purpose, emptied of His Spirit because of the cares of this life.

Please know that this is not intended to bring condemnation to your heart or make you feel like you are failing God. Shut the door to condemnation! This study is to guard against the plot of the enemy and to remind us of his snare and intention to make us lose our oil. Remember the parable Jesus so beautifully and clearly teaches us in Matthew 25:1-13 that we read last week. Read it again and meditate on it. Ask God to help you be like the wise virgins illustrated in this parable.

We must guard the oil at all costs. It will take deliberate efforts on our part. It will cost us time and energy. But guard it we must—for the costs of losing it far outweigh the costs of keeping it.

The Word of God is filled with passages that help and instruct us on how to strengthen our hearts and minds and fight and win against the plot of the enemy—how to shut the door and guard the oil.

For our study, I felt directed to look to the book of Psalms for guidance. The Psalms are a powerful weapon in the hand of the believer. Psalm 1 begins with a portrait of someone with a firm foundation in God and likens that person to a tree planted by the rivers of water. The Psalms conclude with the powerful passage in Psalm 150 that counsels everyone and everything that has breath to praise the Lord. But between Psalm 1 and Psalm 150, we read passages that are emotional and sometimes desperate cries for help. Others are filled with thanksgiving and gratitude to God for His faithfulness and provision. We are also reminded of God's mighty acts and His immeasurable and incomparable greatness throughout the book.

You might say that Psalms reflects the life of every believer. We have experienced both the sorrow and joy and the triumphs and defeats as recorded in the Psalms. But even though we have the emotional highs and lows that sometimes come with life, as we determine to walk with God and have proper perspective and prioritize accordingly, we will be triumphant and shut the door to the schemes of the enemy. We will arrive at the same conclusion that is so beautifully recorded for us—"Let everything that has breath praise the Lord!" We will see His presence make the difference in every area of our life.

Let's look to Psalms for guidance on prioritizing properly. Let's use the insight found in this beloved book to help us guard against an oil leak and shut the door to the enemy's plot.

Read Psalm 139:23 & 24 as we enter this part of our study. Meditate on these verses and ask God to search your heart and bring to light anything that may hinder you from shutting the door to the tactics of the enemy.

> *Search me [thoroughly], O God, and know my heart! Try me and know my thoughts! And see if there is any wicked or hurtful way in me, and lead me in the way everlasting (vv. 23-24).*

Write a prayer asking God to help you improve in areas where you have seen yourself with a possible oil leak. Remember, this

acknowledgment is not to make you feel condemned or guilty. Just the opposite will occur when you honestly address those areas where you have grown lax or complacent. Your joy will be restored and so will your strength. Ask openly for His help. Welcome His presence and guidance. The enemy will see you shut the door to his strategy as you determine to guard your oil. You and everyone in your home and life will be blessed as a result.

_____

_____

_____

_____

_____

_____

_____

_____

_____

Now that we have evaluated our hearts and have prayerfully acknowledged areas we need strengthened, let's look to the Word for guidance in these areas. The Scripture is our life source. Applying it will shut the door to the plot of our enemy and his strategies against us.

Meditate on the following verses and ask God to renew your passion for His presence and for His righteousness. Welcome that hunger and thirst for God in your heart and in your home. Jesus told us in Matthew 5:6, *Blessed are those who hunger and thirst for righteousness, for they shall be filled.* When we truly hunger for Him, we will desire for His presence to be with us and we will make it a priority to seek Him daily! His presence will be a priority in our homes and hearts.

O God, You are my God, earnestly will I seek You; my inner self thirsts for You, my flesh longs and is faint for You, in a dry and weary land where no water is (Ps. 63:1 AMP).

As the deer pants for the water brooks, So pants my soul for You, O God (Ps. 42:1).

Let's look at Psalm 5:3:

In the morning You hear my voice, O Lord; in the morning I prepare [a prayer, a sacrifice for You and watch and wait [for You to speak to my heart] (AMP).

This verse declares that I will speak to the Lord in the morning—in the beginning of my day. I will also take time to listen for Him to respond as He speaks to my heart. Yes, in the hectic world we live in, taking time in the morning for prayer and devotion is certainly easier said than done. But proper priority—first things first—is a powerful way to guard against an oil leak.

<u>*Welcome God in your home with each new day.*</u>
<u>*Make His presence a priority in your schedule!*</u>

Prioritizing properly will cause you to seek Him and set aside time in your home for devotions and prayer. His presence felt in your home will make it much easier to keep your proclamation positive. We tend to guard our words much more carefully when we are mindful of the presence of God.

A familiar verse is found in Psalm 19:14 serves as a reminder on the importance of our words. It's actually a petition asking that our words be acceptable to God.

> *Let the words of my mouth and the meditation of my heart be acceptable in Your sight, O Lord, my [firm, impenetrable] Rock and my Redeemer (AMP).*

This verse serves as a reminder of the importance of our words and our thoughts being acceptable and in alignment with the Word of God and His will for us. This verse alone reminds us of the emphasis we need to place on both the way we think and what we say. Our thoughts and our words are intertwined. Remember the quote I used earlier in reference to our words, "If it's in the well, it's coming up in the bucket."

For my speech to be acceptable to God, it must confirm His Word. I must be careful to declare the truth of what His Word promises, in faith believing He is able to complete what He has said He would do.

> *I will say of the Lord, "He is my refuge and my fortress; My God, in Him I will trust," (Ps. 91:2).*

Pursuing God and seeking His counsel will guard your heart against the snare of the enemy and that dreaded oil leak.

> ***Guarding the oil will enable you to shut the door to the enemy's plot.***

> *Show me Your ways, O Lord; teach me Your paths. Guide me in Your truth and faithfulness and teach me, for You are the God of my salvation; for You [You only and altogether] do I wait [expectantly] all the day long (Ps. 25:4-5 AMP).*

> *One thing I have desired of the Lord, That will I seek: That I may dwell in the house of the Lord All the days*

of my life, To behold the beauty of the Lord, And to inquire in His temple. For in the time of trouble He shall hide me in His pavilion; In the secret place of His tabernacle He shall hide me; He shall set me high upon a rock (Ps. 27:4-5).

I wait for the Lord, my soul waits, And in His word I do hope. My soul waits for the Lord More than those who watch for the morning—Yes, more than those who watch for the morning (Ps. 130:5-6).

A passionate petition reflects your heart's cry and God is moved by it. Read the passages and be encouraged that God hears and answers our cries of distress.

In my distress I called upon the Lord, And cried out to my God; He heard my voice from His temple, And my cry came before Him, even to His ears (Ps. 18:6).

Then they cried out to the Lord in their trouble, And He saved them out of their distresses. He sent His word and healed them, And delivered them from their destructions (Ps. 107:19-20).

Out of the depths I have cried to You, O Lord; Lord, hear my voice! Let Your ears be attentive To the voice of my supplications (Ps. 130:1-2).

Psalms also reminds us that we can know His peace and experience calm that comes from Him when we call upon the Lord. His perfect peace can be mine, even in the storm.

Then they cry out to the Lord in their trouble, And He brings them out of their distresses. He calms the storm,

So that its waves are still. Then they are glad because
they are quiet; So He guides them to their desired haven
(Ps. 107:28-30).

Remember, you were bought with a price. You are valued by God. He loves you with an eternal, unlimited, immeasurable love. You are unique and a one of a kind original. In you are potential and purpose placed there by our Creator.

I will praise You, for I am fearfully and wonderfully
made; Marvelous are Your works, And that my soul
knows very well. My frame was not hidden from You,
When I was made in secret, And skillfully wrought
in the lowest parts of the earth. Your eyes saw my
substance, being yet unformed. And in Your book they
all were written, The days fashioned for me, When as
yet there were none of them. How precious also are
Your thoughts to me, O God! How great is the sum of
them! If I should count them, they would be more in
number than the sand; When I awake, I am still with
You (Ps. 139:14-18).

The devil doesn't want you to even be aware that you are created with potential and purpose. Potential is powerless until utilized. Pray for God to awaken your potential and your desire to walk in His purpose for your life. Having great potential is His gift to you. Using it is your gift to Him. You can and will make a difference in the lives of those you love, and even to some you may never even meet in this life, when you walk in your potential.

We must guard the oil at all costs. It will take deliberate efforts on our part. It will cost us time and energy and require discipline. But remember, guard it we must—for the costs of losing it far outweigh the costs of keeping it!

As you journal this week, spend time in Psalms. Write down your thoughts. Be encouraged through the Word of God and by being in His presence. Be deliberate in your efforts to spend time with God. <u>Your full potential is never fully realized until you routinely spend time in His presence.</u> His presence awakens your potential and purpose. It creates a doorway to your destiny—a pathway to His plan! His plans for your life are better than your dreams.

Meditate on Him and acknowledge the areas that you need to improve upon. Ask for the Holy Spirit to strengthen you. God will lead you and you will guard your oil. And remember, guarding the oil—stopping the leaks—will enable you to <u>shut the door</u> to the enemy's plot, and will also give you the strength to keep it shut.

Shut the Door

WEEK THREE
Presence & Purpose

Discovering Destiny's Doorway

2 Kings 4:8-17

"I will make God's presence priority in my home and heart!"

In week one of our study we discussed the amazing miracle of the widow woman and her two sons as recorded in 2 Kings 4:1-7. We read how the widow woman shut the door to the plot of the enemy and God intervened. Now, we will walk the journey of the Shunammite woman and see how God moved miraculously in her life when she also chose to shut the door to the devastation of the enemy. Her powerful story and testimony of God's faithfulness is found in 2 Kings 4:8-37.

We will see as we read and study this story, that the Shunammite woman had all the important characteristics we discussed in last week's lesson active in her life. We will read and see her determination in action as she shut the door to the enemy's devastation. Her potential surfaced and her purpose prevailed. She had proper perspective throughout her crisis and:

She made God's presence priority in her home and heart.
She made her proclamation positive based
on His Word and promises.
She made her pursuit proactive and was not passive
about God's guidance in her life.
She made her petition passionate as she prayed.
She made her praise powerful because she recognized
God was worthy of her gratitude.
And she experienced His perfect peace in the process of it all.

Now it happened one day that Elisha went to Shunem, where there was a notable woman, and she persuaded him to eat some food. So it was, as often as he passed by, he would turn in there to eat some food. And she said to her husband, "Look now, I know that this is a holy man of God, who passes by us regularly. Please, let us make a small upper room on the wall; and let us put a bed for him there, and a table and a chair and a lampstand; so it will be, whenever he comes to us, he can turn in there," (2 Kings 4:8-10).

> **There are those who are called and walking in obedience to His voice and they are standing in the doorway to their destinies.**

Like the widow woman, she perceived and discerned that Elisha was a holy man of God and her discernment brought forth action on her part. The Shunammite woman knew Elisha brought with him the presence of God. She desired for God to have a place of habitation rather than just a place of visitation in her home. Yes, she welcomed God's presence in her home. *His presence was a priority to her.*

It was because she discerned that Elisha was a holy man of God that she made that deliberate effort to ensure he had a place in her home. This was so important and such a priority to her that she interrupted her schedule and changed her plans to prepare an addition on her house.

It is important that we value God's presence so much that He is free to interrupt our routine and schedule anytime. Seeking His presence should always take precedence and not be just another thing on our list to fit in our busy lifestyles. Remember, first things first. Our actions reflect what is important to us. We must make room for God in our home life. We must make Him first in our heart. We must choose God first over all our choices. He will help us organize our schedule effectively when we give Him first place.

Yes, she deliberately made a personal place of comfort for Elisha and gave him access to come anytime he needed or chose. No doubt, Elisha felt welcomed and at home in her house. As a result, God's presence took up habitation in the Shunammite woman's home.

POINT TO PONDER:

She discerned Elisha was a holy man of God. When someone meets you, do they discern that you have a relationship with God? When they get to know you, do they see you as a disciple and genuine follower of Jesus Christ? It is my prayer that the fruit of the Spirit is readily present in us so that others perceive and know that our relationship with God is genuine. Like the Shunammite woman knew and saw God through Elisha, may others know and see Him through us.

I find it interesting that she called the addition a small upper room. It immediately reminds us of the place of the Holy Spirit outpouring in Acts 2. How important it is for us to have an upper room experience in our walk with God. We know that the faithful followers of Jesus gathered in the upper room in Jerusalem (see Acts 1:12-14) and continued in prayer and supplication until the Day of Pentecost. It was there that they received the infilling of the Holy Spirit. If we have ever needed the power of the Holy Spirit in our lives and homes, it is in these perilous times. We should make every effort to ensure that we have an upper room—a place of sincere prayer and supplication—in our homes. We may not have a literal upper room, but our prayers can create the same atmosphere.

Welcome the Holy Spirit in your house.
Make God's presence a priority in your home.

As the story unfolds, we read that because of the Shunammite woman's faithful and attentive care of Elisha and his servant Gehazi, Elisha wanted to bless her. He sought to find out her heart's desire, a need, or perhaps an unanswered prayer, for which he could seek God on her behalf to repay her for her kindness to them.

> *And it happened one day that he came there, and he turned in to the upper room and lay down there. Then he said to Gehazi his servant, "Call this Shunammite woman." When he had called her, she stood before him. And he said to him, "Say now to her, 'Look, you have been concerned for us with all this care. What can I do for you? Do you want me to speak on your behalf to the king or to the commander of the army?'" She answered, "I dwell among my own people." So he said, "What then is to be done for her?" And Gehazi answered, "Actually, she has no son, and her husband*

is old." So he said, "Call her." When he had called her, she stood in the doorway. Then he said, "About this time next year you shall embrace a son." And she said, "No, my lord. Man of God, do not lie to your maidservant!" (2 Kings 4:11-16)

This passage shows us Elisha's heart concerning the hospitality of this woman. He was resting—abiding comfortably—in her home and was thinking of her kindness and of ways he may repay her. He asked his servant Gehazi to call for her. She came as requested. When asked what she may have need of, she simply replied, "I dwell among my own people." Her response indicated that she was secure and lived among relatives and had no personal needs. This was certainly a stark contrast to the widow woman's story in the first portion of 2 Kings 4. But as the Shunammite woman's story unfolds, we will see that she too, had need of a miracle. God came through for her as well.

We read that Elisha further discussed wanting to show gratitude to her with Gehazi. Gehazi pointed out his observation. He reminded Elisha that she had no son. Her husband was elderly and the hope of having a son had likely been put away by this woman and her husband for some time now. They had given up their dream of having a son and heir.

Elisha called for her the second time. Interestingly, this time the passage says, "she stood in the doorway."

When I studied this passage, I felt as if the Lord spoke to my heart and said that there are those who are called and walking in obedience to His voice and they are standing in the doorway to their destinies. Think of it! This doorway was actually there because of the Shunammite woman's desire to make God's presence a priority in her home. This doorway was constructed because of that desire. Her hunger for God's presence to take up habitation in her home actually created the doorway to her destiny. The same happens with us. When we spend time in God's presence and make it a priority to do so, we become more aware of our own purpose. Our hunger for God and welcoming His presence creates and places us in the doorway to our destiny.

We concluded last week's lesson by reading and meditating on a portion of Psalm 139. Remember, you were created with purpose and a destiny. You are wonderfully made—yes, personally designed—by our Creator. You are loved by God and He has great things planned for your life. He loves you so much that He desires to be with you.

Meditate once more on this comforting passage. Let's read it again, this time in a different version that may give even more insight.

> *You are the one who put me together inside my mother's body, and I praise you because of the wonderful way you created me. Everything you do is marvelous! Of this I have no doubt. Nothing about me is hidden from you! I was secretly woven together deep in the earth below, but with your own eyes you saw my body being formed. Even before I was born, you had written in your book everything I would do. Your thoughts are far beyond my understanding, much more than I could ever imagine. I try to count your thoughts, but they outnumber the grains of sand on the beach. And when I awake, I will find you nearby (Ps. 139:13-18 CEV).*

Another powerful passage that reminds us of God's intimate love and care for us is found in Jeremiah 29:11-13. When you read this passage it is as if you are hearing the heart of God toward you. It also reminds us of the importance and the benefits of being in His presence through communing with Him in prayer.

For I know the thoughts that I think toward you, says the Lord, thoughts of peace and not of evil, to give you a future and a hope. Then you will call upon Me and go and pray to Me, and I will listen to you. And you will seek Me and find Me, when you search for Me with all your heart (vv.11-13).

Take a moment and think on these passages we have just read. How does it make you feel to know that God loves you and has specific plans for you? So often we spend so much effort and energy in seeking our purpose instead of the One Who created us on purpose with a purpose. Instead, we should search for Him with all of our hearts. It's when we find Him that we find our real purpose. Being in His presence is where we find direction and details for our life's choices.

Lean on, trust in, and be confident in the Lord with all your heart and mind and do not rely on your own insight or understanding. In all your ways know, recognize, and acknowledge Him, and He will direct and make straight and plain your paths (Prov. 3:5-6 AMP).

The more time we spend in His presence, the more we know and love Him. And the more we know and love Him, the more we are assured we can trust Him. Being in His presence brings assurance, comfort, and peace. It gives us an awareness of His love and protection. It provides clarity to our purpose and gives direction for our choices. How important it is to make His presence a priority!

Pray and ask God to make you more intent than ever to be in His presence daily.

POINT TO PONDER:

Think on this thought again: Be deliberate in your efforts to spend time with God. Your full potential is never fully realized until you routinely spend time in His presence. His presence awakens your potential and purpose. It creates a doorway to your destiny—a pathway to His plan. His plans for your life are better than your dreams.

Yes, shut the door to the enemy and watch God place you in the doorway to your destiny!

Elisha gave a very direct prophecy over this woman. He spoke as she stood in the doorway and declared about this time next year you shall embrace a son. When we stand in the doorway we gain insight and a glimpse of the vision for what is beyond the open door before us.

But her response indicated that she felt this prophecy was too good to be true. She responded by saying, "No, my lord. Man of God, do not lie to your maidservant!"

She no doubt had hoped for and prayed over and over for a son. She had her heart's desire set on this many times only to be disappointed. And disappointment, especially repeat disappointment, can often cause someone to give up. The pain of hoping over and over again, only to suffer another delay, makes us want to shut our minds and hopes to the possibilities we've prayed would be a reality. It seems sometimes it's less painful to dismiss our dream than to suffer disappointment yet again.

The word "disappoint" means *to thwart or defeat the expectation or hope of something*. The enemy desires to cause you to doubt God's promises or prophetic words spoken to you. When that happens disappointment sets in and you find yourself with a sick heart. Your heart is sick because your expectation dies and as a result hope is defeated.

Read Proverbs 13:12 and write down your thoughts concerning it:

> *Hope deferred makes the heart sick, but when the desire is fulfilled, it is a tree of life (AMP).*

_____

_____

_____

_____

_____

_____

_____

_____

_____

Have you ever hoped for something so much only to suffer disappointment over and over again? Have you prayed for someone you love and they still are making poor choices that cause themselves and those that love them so much pain? Have you suffered physically and are in need of a miracle? Have your hopes been crushed repeatedly by Satan's plot? Have you just quit thinking of it all because it hurts too much to hope anymore?

I believe this was the case with the Shunammite woman concerning her hopes for a son. But in spite of her lack of hope, her faithfulness and desire for God's presence created a doorway to her destiny. An appointment was made for her promise to arrive!

> *But the woman conceived, and bore a son when the appointed time had come, of which Elisha had told her (2 Kings 4:17).*

Just as Elisha prophesied, the woman conceived and bore a son when the appointed time had come. God's timing and ours are often not the same. But God is faithful and He will perform what He has promised.

I often say and will again now that truth always overrides the facts! The facts often say one thing but His truth declares another. Look at these powerful verses about God and His promises concerning us.

> *God is not a man, that He should tell or act a lie, neither the son of man, that He should feel repentance or compunction [for what He has promised]. Has He said and shall He not do it? Or has He spoken and shall He not make it good? (Num. 23:19 AMP)*

> *Heaven and earth will pass away, but My words will by no means pass away (Luke 21:33).*

> *God cannot tell lies! And so his promises and vows are two things that can never be changed. We have run to God for safety. Now his promises should greatly encourage us to take hold of the hope that is right in front of us (Heb. 6:18 CEV).*

Think of these passages you've just read. Meditate on how powerful our God is. Rejoice because He is true and faithful to His Word. Take time at this point in our study to shut the door to doubt and painful disappointment by praising God for His faithfulness. In the appointed time, He will be faithful to complete what He has promised you.

Write a prayer of praise and thanksgiving for the promises God has made. In that prayer, give Him praise for remaining faithful to His Word. Express your faith in His ability to perform what He has promised. You will begin to feel that doorway to your destiny opening and your disappointment fading in the assurance and hope of what is ahead.

_____

_____

_____

_____

_____

_____

_____

_____

Your declaration of your faith in God and His ability to do what He has promised will enable you to shut the door to doubt and disappointment.

Let's consider the words again in 2 Kings 4:17, *But the woman conceived, and bore a son when the appointed time had come, of which Elisha had told her.*

When the appointed time had come—that makes my heart rejoice! Just because it hasn't happened yet doesn't mean it's not on the way. Your appointed time is coming. Your appointed time is scheduled with God. God's word is true. He is faithful to His promises.

Let's look at a powerful and familiar verse concerning the appointed time of God's promises:

For the vision is yet for an appointed time and it hastens to the end [fulfillment]; it will not deceive or disappoint. Though it tarry, wait [earnestly] for it, because it will surely come; it will not be behindhand on its appointed day (Hab. 2:3 AMP).

I love this verse. It also reminds us that the appointed time is coming. The vision—the promise—it will be fulfilled and it will not deceive or disappoint when it comes.

How do I not lose hope while waiting for the appointed time? What do I do in the meantime while I wait for the promise? I always say, "The meantime is *mean* time!" No one likes to wait.

How do I shut the door to the enemy's attempt to drain my heart of expectation and hope while waiting—especially when the wait is long? The answer: I spend time in His presence and I feed my soul and mind with the Word of God. And when I do, I find my hope revived. When my hope is alive and my expectations are rekindled, I can truly look ahead with excitement for the fulfillment of my destiny and purpose in God. My mindset is changed. My hope is restored and my heart is no longer sick. Instead, my disappointment is dismissed in anticipation of my appointment with destiny. And when I walk in expectation—I not only look forward with excitement—I actually enjoy my journey getting there.

Reading and applying the Word of God daily changes our mindset.

> *And do not be conformed to this world, but be transformed by the renewing of your mind, that you may prove what is that good and acceptable and perfect will of God (Rom. 12:2).*

This verse reminds us to think differently. Allow the Word of God and His presence to renew your mind. Think and meditate on the truth of God's Word. Shut the door to the current pain of your circumstances by focusing on His promises. If my focus is where I am, then where I am is likely where I will stay. We must look beyond the moment, persuaded and confident that God is working all things for our good.

We are assured and know that [God being a partner in their labor] all things work together and are [fitting into a plan] for good to and for those who love God and are called according to [His] design and purpose (Rom. 8:28 AMP).

Read and purpose in your heart to follow the directions given in these verses:

Wait and hope for and expect the Lord; be brave and of good courage and let your heart be stout and enduring. Yes, wait for and hope for and expect the Lord (Ps. 27:14 AMP).

I wait for the Lord, I expectantly wait, and in His word do I hope (Ps. 130:5 AMP).

We are to be brave and courageous with full expectation that God will come through for us. We are to look ahead beyond the moment, confident, watching and waiting, for the promises of God to become a reality in our lives. And when we do, we shut the door to disappointment and dread. Even in our waiting we are assured it will happen just as He promised!

Hope is not just something a believer does—hope is something a believer has.

This verse in Micah is one of my favorites. It makes it personal. As for me, it declares, I will look to the Lord! I will be confident in Him. I will watch with expectation. I am waiting, fully believing God will do what He said. He is hearing and listening to my heart's cry.

But as for me, I will look to the Lord and confident in Him I will keep watch; I will wait with hope and expectancy for the God of my salvation; my God will hear me (Micah 7:7 AMP).

Take a moment and praise God for His faithfulness.
Praise Him for renewed hope and confident
expectation in your heart.
Believe Him for your appointed time.
<u>Shut the door</u> to disappointment in anticipation of
your appointment.
Wait with hope and expectancy.
For God is faithful to keep His promises.

The Shunammite woman made God's presence a priority. She was deliberate in her desire to make God welcome in her home. She made a place for Him to dwell. She wanted Him to have a place of habitation. She didn't want just an occasional visitation by God.

The results were amazing! By making God's presence a priority, she created a doorway to her destiny. Hope was revived and her expectation for the future was bright again. She <u>shut the door</u> to dread and disappointment. And her appointed time came. So will yours.

Pray and ask God to help you to always make His presence a priority. Set aside a special time with Him each day. Ask God to help you not become distracted with your routine and schedule and lose sight of what matters most. Being in His presence brings renewed joy and purpose.

In His presence, the enemy's doors of disappointment are shut and the doorway to our destiny is revealed!

Declare with renewed determination:

"I will make God's presence priority in my home and heart!"

Shut the Door

WEEK FOUR

Proclaim & Pursue

Running To God

2 Kings 4:18-26

"I will make my proclamation positive based on His Word and promises!"

"I will make my pursuit proactive and will not be passive about God's guidance in my life!"

Let's begin this week's study with some strong instructions found in the book of James before we continue with the story of the Shunammite woman. Now, you know that by these passages

Endurance and wisdom are needed when we are in warfare.

being chosen to open this week's study that—well, trouble is on the way for our friend from Shunem.

We concluded last week's study excited about her appointed time and her renewed hope and purpose. But you don't expect the enemy to leave her alone in her victory, do you? He won't leave us alone either. That is why we have to seek God and be mindful of the enemy's plot at all times. We have to be on guard and ready to shut the door to his manipulation and methods.

If we are honest, James is a book that we would sometimes rather study to teach someone else than to learn a lesson from it and apply it to ourselves. It's strong medicine! It contains passages that are sometimes easier to offer advice from that to take.

> *My brethren, count it all joy when you fall into various trials, knowing that the testing of your faith produces patience. But let patience have its perfect work, that you may be perfect and complete, lacking nothing. If any of you lacks wisdom, let him ask of God, who gives to all liberally and without reproach, and it will be given to him. But let him ask in faith, with no doubting, for he who doubts is like a wave of the sea driven and tossed by the wind. For let not that man suppose that he will receive anything from the Lord; he is a double-minded man, unstable in all his ways (James 1:2-8).*

Let's read it again in the Contemporary English Version for even more clarity:

> *My friends, be glad, even if you have a lot of trouble. You know that you learn to endure by having your faith tested. But you must learn to endure everything, so that you will be completely mature and not lacking in anything. If any of you need wisdom, you should*

ask God, and it will be given to you. God is generous and won't correct you for asking. But when you ask for something, you must have faith and not doubt. Anyone who doubts is like an ocean wave tossed around in a storm. If you are that kind of person, you can't make up your mind, and you surely can't be trusted. So don't expect the Lord to give you anything at all (CEV).

Wow! That's straightforward. *Be glad when you have trouble!* What? But James goes on to explain why he says what he says. It's through those times of testing that we learn endurance. And when we learn endurance, we become mature and lack nothing.

He goes on to say that if you need wisdom (I certainly do!), simply ask God for it. He will give it.

Imagine if your child—especially as a teenager or young adult—came before you and sincerely sought your advice and wisdom on a matter. Any matter! You would stop what you were doing and gladly give instructions. As His children, God greatly desires to give us guidance, wisdom, and instruction. And when we ask He is more than willing to guide us.

When we receive promises from God and take them to heart, the enemy wants to bring distractions to our lives in hopes of delaying us from receiving them, or misdirect us from the path we are on to God's purpose.

So, endurance and wisdom are needed when we are in warfare. As we continue with the story of the Shunammite woman we will see that she has both!

Let's go back to her story and see what happens next.

And the child grew. Now it happened one day that he went out to his father, to the reapers. And he said to his father, "My head, my head!" So he said to a servant,

*"Carry him to his mother." When he had taken him
and brought him to his mother, he sat on her knees till
noon, and then died (2 Kings 4:18-20).*

What? Does this even make sense? She had finally received her
promise! She had loved and nurtured her son and watched him
grow. Now, in a moment, everything changed. How can this be?

Do you have reasons to feel the same way about circumstances
in your life? Did you wait for what seemed like a lifetime for a
promise, a prophecy, or a prayer to be realized—only to have it
seemingly lost or taken away in one instant?

Perhaps you have a ministry that God entrusted to your care
and you were so overjoyed in the beginning to be a part of it. You
watched it grow and it seemed healthy and you were excited about
where it appeared to be going. Now it is struggling and looks like
it might even come to an untimely and unexpected end.

Maybe you have a son or daughter, a family member or loved
one, and you were elated when they finally gave their life to Christ.
You were so thankful as you saw everything beginning to change
for their good. But now they are floundering in their walk with
God and you are fearful they may regress into former sins. Your
hope is fighting to stay alive as you witness their struggles.

Maybe you're battling emotional pain because of hurt inflicted
on you by someone you love. Betrayal by a loved one or friend can
cause deep wounds. You try and hide it but the pain is very real
and is weighing on you constantly. The demise of a relationship
hurts.

Perhaps you are suffering with a physical illness that is draining
your strength. You truly want to work for God and live a productive
life with and for your loved ones. But you are battling daily with
sickness and it's hard to even enjoy life as you once did. Your hopes
and plans are shattered because of your physical problems.

Possibly, you are fighting a financial battle and can't pay your debts or meet the needs of your family or even yourself. Your job fell through or your salary was reduced. Or perhaps you just planned poorly and now your outgo exceeds your income. You are weary from the stress of it all.

All of these situations can cause the death of a dream or vision!

There are four arenas in which the enemy loves to do battle against us: spiritually, emotionally, physically, and financially. Maybe you are in a battle in one or more or even *all* of these places. It feels that you are struggling just to keep your promises alive. You can relate to the Shunammite woman's story. Life has taken an unexpected turn and now your heart is breaking.

There is so much to this story that isn't recorded. Her son, still very young, but old enough to want to watch his dad work in the fields, became instantly ill and died in her arms in a matter of a few hours.

I can imagine that when the servant brought him home to her that this loving mother immediately stopped what she was doing. Her crisis just came in the door. *Nothing else seemed important.* When your crisis comes home you feel the same way.

Her focus changed and her agenda was no longer important. She held her son and prayed for him and attempted in every way to comfort him. And still…he died in her arms. What a seemingly tragic and heartbreaking conclusion of what started out as such a joyful promise.

We can be free from the heavy weight of our burden by giving it to God. He will in turn sustain us.

What she does next is amazing to me every time I read it. Let's read this verse and see her response to what had just happened.

> *And she went up and laid him on the bed of the man of*
> *God, <u>shut the door</u> upon him, and went out (2 Kings*
> *4:21).*

She went up—up to the upper room! She laid her son's lifeless body on the bed of the man of God, the place where the anointing rested, and <u>shut the door.</u>

What an example to all of us! Remember, we discussed earlier the importance of having an upper room atmosphere in our home. Our home should be a place that is saturated with the presence of God. It should be a place where prayers and supplications to Him are made daily. It can then be a place where we can easily and readily cast our cares—our broken dreams and plans—at His feet.

But she didn't stop there. After she <u>shut the door,</u> she embarked on a journey in pursuit of God!

In the Old Testament, we know that the prophets were powerfully used and anointed of God. Miracles were wrought through them as they walked in obedience to Him. It is no wonder that this determined mother set out to find Elisha. After all, he was the one God used to speak the prophecy concerning her son. Now, surely God would use him to bring life again to her promise.

I am to speak words that build faith—including my own.

> *Then she called to her husband, and said, "Please send*
> *me one of the young men and one of the donkeys, that*
> *I may run to the man of God and come back." So he*
> *said, "Why are you going to him today? It is neither*
> *the New Moon nor the Sabbath." And she said, "It is*
> *well," (2 Kings 4:22-23).*

Again I ask—what? This doesn't make sense either! She had just witnessed the death of her son. She had taken his lifeless body and carefully placed it in the bed of the anointed prophet. And now she is proclaiming, "It is well." It would seem it was anything but well in her world. But she had taken her situation and left her problem in the upper room—in the place of the anointing. And she shut the door. She didn't engage in conversation that could have altered her focus on her mission to find God. She was determined. She wasn't wasting a moment of her time.

POINT TO PONDER:

<u>Be careful who you converse with when in a crisis.</u> It's important at times to share with a fellow prayer warrior or a person of like faith. But don't be careless and share your burdens with just anyone. Even some caring people are capable of speaking death and doubt over you. Shut the door to the naysayers! Listen to those who agree with you in faith.

Let's look at a familiar passage that we have all leaned upon in our walk with God.

> *Casting the whole of your care [all your anxieties, all your worries, all your concerns, once and for all] on Him, for He cares for you affectionately and cares about you watchfully (1 Pet. 5:7 AMP).*

This is a powerful reminder to us! We are to do just as she did. We are to take our burdens to the Lord and leave them with Him. When we place them in His capable hands we can shut the door to worry, fear, and anxiety. God is not only capable of handling our crisis, but He cares for us affectionately and watches over us continually.

Now look at another instruction with a wonderful promise.

> *Cast your burden on the Lord [releasing the weight of*

> *it] and He will sustain you; He will never allow the [consistently] righteous to be moved (made to slip, fall, or fail) (Ps. 55:22 AMP).*

Praise God! This verse is so powerful. It reminds us that we can be free from the heavy weight of our burden by giving it to God. He in turn will sustain us. He will never allow His faithful children to fail when we give Him our problems and concerns.

Once we have truly given our burdens to the Lord and shut the door to our circumstances, our focus changes. We are able to think clearly and focus on the truth of God's Word. Then our words reflect what is going on in our heart. Like the Shunammite woman, when faith takes hold where the enemy thought he had a grip—we can also declare in the face of our greatest conflict, "It is well!"

When faith takes a grip—the enemy loses his!

Why is it so important that our words are positive? Faith comes by hearing, and our own heart and mind hear us first. Let your ears hear your voice declare truth. Your faith will increase. We are to speak life and not death. Faith and not fear! *We can alter our own mindset by what we hear ourselves declare.*

> *So faith comes by hearing [what is told], and what is heard comes by the preaching [of the message that came from the lips] of Christ (the Messiah Himself) (Rom. 10:17 AMP).*

I am to speak words that build faith—including my own. Those faith building words come from the Word of God. Read the Word of God. Digest it. Live it and speak it. It is Living Bread from God to our souls.

"I will make my proclamation positive based on His Word and promises!"

Let's read some of the Scriptures in Proverbs that instruct us on the importance of saying the right thing at the right time.

> *Death and life are in the power of the tongue, and they who indulge in it shall eat the fruit of it [for death or life] (Prov. 18:21 AMP).*

So often, we speak the negative (death) rather than life (God's promises) over our situation. We need to ask God to help us to be one who always speaks life. We need to declare by faith with a positive proclamation, "It is well!"

> *In a multitude of words transgression is not lacking, but he who restrains his lips is prudent (Prov. 10:19 AMP).*

This verse reminds us that when we talk too much, sin results. If we are not careful with our words, we can destroy someone's character or self-worth by our careless words, especially when we are stirred by our emotions. Not only that, we can destroy our own faith by talking too much about our dilemma.

> *Anxiety in a man's heart weighs it down, but an encouraging word makes it glad (Prov. 12:25 AMP).*

What a powerful reminder that one encouraging word can cause someone's heart that is weighed down to be glad. Ask God to let you encourage others—and yourself—with words of truth and promise that make hearts glad.

A man has joy in making an apt answer, and a word spoken at the right moment—how good it is! (Prov. 15:23 AMP).

This verse simply says that giving the right answer at the right time makes everyone happy. Both the speaker and the hearer rejoice.

Pleasant words are as a honeycomb, sweet to the mind and healing to the body (Prov. 16:24 AMP).

Pleasant words are sweet and enjoyed by all. They bring joy to our thoughts and healing to our body.

A word fitly spoken and in due season is like apples of gold in settings of silver (Prov. 25:11 AMP).

This simply paints a beautiful picture of words spoken correctly.

Take a moment and write a prayer asking for guidance with your words. Just from Proverbs alone, we see the value and benefit of speaking with a positive proclamation. Our words make a difference every day and in all situations, both for the speaker and the hearer.

_____

_____

_____

_____

_____

_____

_____

_____

_____

[The Servant of God says] The Lord God has given Me the tongue of a disciple and of one who is taught, that I should know how to speak a word in season to him who is weary. He wakens Me morning by morning, He wakens My ear to hear as a disciple [as one who is taught] (Isa. 50:4 AMP).

What a beautiful verse concerning the importance of speaking the right words.

In a world that is filled with those who are hurting and needing answers, there has never been a time when we needed more to realize the importance and the power of speaking life and not death. One declaration of truth to a weary fellow believer may be just the word of encouragement they need to make it through their trial. One kind word to a broken spirit may be all that is needed to set them on the right path to restoration. Proclaiming truth and God's promises in the face of your own fear will cause your faith to take hold and the enemy to lose his grip.

What a difference a positive proclamation makes!

POINT TO PONDER:

Words are powerful indeed. They can build up the weak and tear down the strong. When I speak, my motive should be pure. My method should be love. My means should be grace. If what I intend to say has impure motives, then I shouldn't say it. If I can't say it in love, then I should be quiet. If I cannot season it with grace, then it will be ineffective. We should always be aware of the power of the spoken word. And we should use that power for the right reason—to build up, not to tear down!

Not only did the Shunammite woman demonstrate that she had a positive proclamation, she was determined to pursue God. In the face of her greatest challenge she spoke in faith and passionately pursued God's presence.

> *Then she saddled a donkey, and said to her servant, "Drive, and go forward; do not slacken the pace for me unless I tell you." And so she departed, and went to the man of God at Mount Carmel. So it was, when the man of God saw her afar off, that he said to his servant Gehazi, "Look, the Shunammite woman! Please run now to meet her, and say to her, 'Is it well with you? Is it well with your husband? Is it well with the child?'" And she answered, "It is well," (2 Kings 4:24-26).*

I can only visualize this part of the story with the imagination I have been given. You may see it completely differently. But somehow I don't think this affluent woman from Shunem was accustomed to saddling her own donkey. She was in a determined state of mind. She didn't want anything or anyone to hinder her from getting to Elisha. This servant probably stood in amazement at her demeanor and determination. And he had no idea why she was in this determined mindset. After all, she had just declared, "It is well"—everything is all right—to her husband.

I like to imagine what it must have looked like even from a distance to Elisha when he saw her hurriedly coming toward him. She was out of her element and was not the least bit worried about proper protocol. She was on a mission and it showed, even from afar!

Elisha sent Gehazi to meet her. When Gehazi asked how she was, she answered again, "It is well!" Her proclamation remained positive but her pursuit of God was proactive.

"I will make my pursuit proactive and will not be passive about God's guidance in my life!"

Have you ever met someone who was holding on to the promises of God, and maybe even saying the right things, but their pursuit of God and His presence was waning? As powerful as our words are, they are not enough. As necessary as it is for us to speak the truth, we must also seek *the* Truth. Jesus is the Way and the Truth and the Life! Without a relationship with Him, our words, even if they are true, are hollow. We must know God and serve Him in order for His words and promises to be effective in our lives. Quoting the Word of God alone isn't enough. Picking favorite verses and claiming them as your own will not suffice without a relationship with Jesus. He is the Word made flesh. To know Him and live for Him activates the power of His word in us.

Read these verses from the Book of John.

> *And the Word became flesh and dwelt among us, and we beheld His glory, the glory as of the only begotten of the Father, full of grace and truth (1:14).*

> *Jesus said to him, I am the Way and the Truth and the Life; no one comes to the Father except by (through) Me (14:6 AMP).*

> *If you live in Me [abide vitally united to Me] and My words remain in you and continue to live in your hearts, ask whatever you will, and it shall be done for you. When you bear (produce) much fruit, My Father is honored and glorified, and you show and prove yourselves to be true followers of Mine (15:7-8 AMP).*

After reading these, why do you think it is important to both pursue God with all of your heart and speak His word over your

life and circumstances? Both are vital to our Christian walk.
Journal your thoughts on this:

_____

_____

_____

_____

_____

_____

_____

_____

Speaking the Word is powerful when you have a relationship with the Word Who became flesh. When you walk in covenant with Christ, His word in you is alive. It is a powerful weapon in the hand of the believer.

To know God, I must actively and consistently pursue a relationship with Him.

> *One thing have I asked of the Lord, that will I seek,*
> *inquire for, and [insistently] require: that I may dwell*
> *in the house of the Lord [in His presence] all the days of*
> *my life, to behold and gaze upon the beauty [the sweet*
> *attractiveness and the delightful loveliness] of the Lord*
> *and to meditate, consider, and inquire in His temple*
> *(Ps. 27:4 AMP).*

POINT TO PONDER:

During the time of preparing this study, I have had many unexpected personal battles arise, and some have been fierce. I have felt pressed on every side. I have asked God to help me in these very areas we are discussing in *Shut the Door*. As I began preparing to write this study, I felt the Lord asked me a question in a time of prayer and meditation, "Will you be the same in your time of pressing as you are in your time of blessing?"

I wanted to respond with a resounding yes, but I felt His Spirit gently reminding me that I must be prepared to put to test some of the very things I am teaching through this study. In my own battles, even now as I write, I am asking God to allow me to always have a teachable spirit that will enable me to practice what I preach. When we are pressed, what is in us is what comes forth. I desire to pursue God as never before in the heat of my battles. I desire that my words be life-giving, for the sake of those I know and love and so that my own faith will increase. I want praise to come forth from my heart when I am on the mountain or in the deepest valley. I want to be able to say without reservation that I am the same in word and in deed during my times of pressing just as I am in my times of blessing. The Shunammite woman is certainly an example we can follow. I pray that others will be able to say the same about us.

Expressing your petition passionately helps you to truly give it to God and release it to His capable care.

In this week's study, we have discussed the importance of a positive proclamation and a proactive pursuit of God. The Shunammite woman had both. She shut the door to the scheme and plot of the enemy. She proclaimed truth and not facts. She pursued God with determination.

As you study this week, be mindful to ask God to increase your awareness of your words. Be constantly aware of what you say both for your sake and those hearing you. Ask Him to help you always pursue His presence and seek His counsel in times of blessing and times of pressing.

Because you pursue Him and declare His Word, no matter what you face, you will also be able to proclaim, "It is well!" And it will be.

I will make my proclamation positive
based on His Word and promises!
I will make my pursuit proactive and will not be
passive about God's guidance in my life!

WEEK FIVE

Petition & Praise

Warrior Arise

2 Kings 4:27-37

"I will make my petition passionate and I will pray as the Holy Spirit leads!"

"I will make my praise powerful because my God is worthy and my heart is grateful!"

The definition of a warrior includes this description: "a person of demonstrated courage, fortitude, zeal." We will see as we continue the story of the Shunammite woman that she definitely demonstrates these characteristics.

It is my prayer that as we determine to shut the door to the enemy in our lives that we too take on these characteristics and run this race as that of a warrior.

In our lesson last week, we saw the determination of this mother as she, in the face of her greatest battle, maintained a positive proclamation and had a very proactive pursuit of God. She shut the door to the plot of the enemy and set out to seek Elisha. We will take up her story this week in 2 Kings 4:27-37.

> *Now when she came to the man of God at the hill, she caught him by the feet, but Gehazi came near to push her away. But the man of God said, "Let her alone; for her soul is in deep distress, and the Lord has hidden it from me, and has not told me." So she said, "Did I ask a son of my lord? Did I not say, 'Do not deceive me?'"* (vv. 27-28)

This portion of the story reveals the brokenness and grief of this mother's heart. All of her fears are revealed and her appeal is passionate. She is transparent with Elisha. To this point, she has guarded her words carefully, but now she is in the presence of the man of God. He is the one she believes will intercede and speak on her behalf to God. She is honest and hides nothing from him. Her words to Elisha were saying to him, *I was afraid it was too good to be true! I was afraid it wouldn't last!*

When we come into the presence of the Lord and pour our hearts out in passionate prayer and supplication to God, it is so important that we are honest and transparent with Him. He knows our pain. He knows our brokenness. He wants to mend our hurts. He is our Heavenly Father. He is our provider. He desires to minister to us in our sorrow. Expressing your petition passionately helps you to truly give it to God and release it to His capable care.

Remember, be careful who you converse with when in a crisis. Yes, share with a fellow prayer warrior or a person of like faith. But don't be careless and share your burdens with just anyone. But when you are in the presence of our omniscient, omnipotent, omnipresent God, attempt to hide nothing from Him. He knows all and is all powerful and is a very present help in your time of need. He knows that your heart hurts and the burden is heavy. Giving it to Him will release you from the weight of it. Let's read this verse again. It is one of my most cherished reminders of His faithfulness in my time of crisis.

> *Cast your burden on the Lord [releasing the weight of it] and He will sustain you; He will never allow the [consistently] righteous to be moved (made to slip, fall, or fail) (Ps. 55:22 AMP).*

Be passionate when you pray. Express your needs to God fervently. When you do, you are releasing your burden and the weight of it to the One Who is more than capable of taking it and turning it around. That's why this Shunammite woman was determined to get to Elisha. We must be determined to take our burdens to the Lord and leave them with Him.

Let's look at this passage concerning prayer:

> *Is anyone among you suffering? Let him pray. Is anyone cheerful? Let him sing psalms. Is anyone among you sick? Let him call for the elders of the church, and let them pray over him, anointing him with oil in the name of the Lord. And the prayer of faith will save the sick, and the Lord will raise him up. And if he has committed sins, he will be forgiven. Confess your trespasses to one another, and pray for one another, that you may be healed. The effective, fervent prayer of a righteous man avails much. Elijah was a man with a nature like ours, and he prayed earnestly that it would not rain; and it did not rain on the land for three years and six months. And he prayed again, and the heaven gave rain, and the earth produced its fruit (James 5:13-18).*

This passage is worthy of considerable thought and discussion. James reminds us here of important truths that apply to all believers. As you journal and study this week, take time to really ponder and search out commentaries on these verses.

Pay close attention to verse 17. It is fascinating to think of Elijah as a man with a nature like our own. He was subject to fear and dread. He knew what it felt like to be disappointed. He had experienced anger. He knew the pain of rejection. He knew his own faults and failures. He even woke up some days tired, not feeling like or wanting to do anything. He was mere flesh and blood with both strengths and weaknesses. Yet, the Spirit within him was powerful and when he prayed amazing things happened.

Yes, the effectual, fervent, passionate prayer of a believer—someone like you or me—led by the Holy Spirit, brings forth great results.

> *Our Shunammite woman was one with*
> *an effectual and fervent prayer.*
> *She was passionate when making her petition.*

Now let's look in the book of Romans concerning prayer. This is another familiar passage that is worthy of taking the time to study and fully understand. This powerful passage reminds us that in those difficult and hard-to-understand places we sometimes face, the Holy Spirit will pray for and through us. When we don't know what to say, when we feel we don't have the right words to pray effectively, this is a great comfort to know the Holy Spirit wil pray for us.

> *So too the [Holy] Spirit comes to our aid and bears us*
> *up in our weakness; for we do not know what prayer*
> *to offer nor how to offer it worthily as we ought, but*

the Spirit Himself goes to meet our supplication and pleads in our behalf with unspeakable yearnings and groanings too deep for utterance. And He Who searches the hearts of men knows what is in the mind of the [Holy] Spirit [what His intent is], because the Spirit intercedes and pleads [before God] in behalf of the saints according to and in harmony with God's will (Rom. 8:26-27 AMP).

And we all love Romans 8:28! This verse is the result of a passionate petition by a believer who is a determined warrior with courage, fortitude, and zeal. Let the warrior in you arise. Don't be passive in your prayer life. Don't be daunted by the enemy's strategy to distract you. Shut the door to his schemes and pray with passion. The results of those prayers are found in this wonderful verse.

We are assured and know that [God being a partner in their labor] all things work together and are [fitting into a plan] for good to and for those who love God and are called according to [His] design and purpose (AMP).

When the devil comes knocking on your door with discouraging words of gloom and dread in an attempt to keep you from passionately petitioning God in prayer, shut the door in his face! Remembering Romans 8:31 & 32 will help you shut that door.

What then shall we say to [all] this? If God is for us, who [can be] against us? [Who can be our foe, if God is on our side?] He who did not withhold or spare [even] His own Son but gave Him up for us all, will He not also with Him freely and graciously give us all [other] things? (AMP)

Praise God! Yes, God is for us so everyone and everything that is against us are just wasting their time, talents, energy, and resources. No power or weapon fashioned can stand against our God. We are on the winning side!

God gave us His Son. How much more will He freely give us the other things we need. He is more than able and willing to come to your aid. Never hesitate to bring your petitions to Him.

This passage in 1 John 5:14-15 also reminds us of the assurance we have that our prayers will be heard and answered when we pray according to His will.

> *And this is the confidence (the assurance, the privilege of boldness) which we have in Him: [we are sure] that if we ask anything (make any request) according to His will (in agreement with His own plan), He listens to and hears us. And if (since) we [positively] know that He listens to us in whatever we ask, we also know [with settled and absolute knowledge] that we have [granted us as our present possessions] the requests made of Him (AMP).*

What about these passages encourage you to want to pray with passion and bring your every need to God?

_____

_____

_____

_____

_____

_____

_____

_____

_____

***Ask God to help you to have determination and
tenacity to pray passionately.
Let the prayer warrior in you arise.
The results will be worth it!***

Let's look now back to our story:

> *Then he said to Gehazi, "Get yourself ready, and take
> my staff in your hand, and be on your way. If you meet
> anyone, do not greet him; and if anyone greets you,
> do not answer him; but lay my staff on the face of the
> child." And the mother of the child said, "As the Lord
> lives, and as your soul lives, I will not leave you." So he
> arose and followed her (2 Kings 4:29-30).*

Elisha sees on her face and hears in her voice the passion in
her petition. He gives immediate instructions to Gehazi and sends
him on his way. But this mother will not settle. She doesn't want
a substitute. She wants the real thing. She wants Elisha to go to
her house. She looks into his eyes with a determination that moves
him to action. She declares with stern sincerity that she will not
leave without him, so he gets up and follows her.

I love that her determination moved the prophet into action.
Elisha had sent his servant in his stead but his plans changed
because of her passionate plea. Imagine how our loving God is
moved into action on our behalf when we come to Him with that
kind of passion. God recognizes those who love and trust Him,
and that love and trust is always rewarded with His sweet presence.

> *The Lord is good, a Strength and Stronghold in the
> day of trouble; He knows (recognizes, has knowledge
> of, and understands) those who take refuge and trust
> in Him (Nahum 1:7 AMP).*

God knows, recognizes, has knowledge of, and understands those who seek and trust in Him. He is a Strength and a Stronghold in our day of trouble. The Shunammite woman ran to God with her passionate petition. And we must always do the same! Her actions demonstrated her complete trust in God's ability to turn things around.

Trust in God is always recognized by Him and the results of that trust are powerful.

> Commit your way to the Lord [roll and repose each care of your load on Him]; trust (lean on, rely on, and be confident) also in Him and He will bring it to pass (Ps. 37:5 AMP).

He wants nothing in us hurting or broken. He doesn't want to just repair portions of us.

So, Elisha returned to the home of the Shunammite with this determined mother and prayer warrior. Of course this was a familiar and comfortable place for him to enter. It was Elisha's home away from home. She had made it such. As we discussed earlier, this faithful woman of God knew the importance of God's presence abiding in her home. His presence in this house was about to change everything.

> Now Gehazi went on ahead of them, and laid the staff on the face of the child; but there was neither voice nor hearing. Therefore he went back to meet him, and told him, saying, "The child has not awakened." When Elisha came into the house, there was the child, lying dead on his bed. He went in therefore, shut the door behind the two of them, and prayed to the Lord (2 Kings 4:31-33).

We read in this passage that Gehazi had gone on ahead as instructed but nothing happened as a result. The child was still lifeless on the bed of the man of God. But when Elisha came into the house, he went in and shut the door behind the two of them.

He did the same thing the Shunammite woman had done. He did the same thing he had instructed earlier for the widow woman to do. He shut the door! He closed out all distractions to focus entirely on his God.

POINT TO PONDER:

As we have already discussed, so often we are plagued with heavy agendas and distractions on every side. The purpose of this study is to help us focus on what really matters and shut the door to those things that hinder and oppose the will of God in our lives. We must shut out all that is wrong and bring in with us those things that are eternal.

Both this mother and the widow woman's sons were inside with them. Our families cannot feel they are shut out of our lives to accommodate a busy lifestyle. It doesn't mean that there are not other things of importance in your life, but never let your family feel as if they are not as important to you as the next thing on your to-do list.

> *And he went up and lay on the child, and put his mouth on his mouth, his eyes on his eyes, and his hands on his hands; and he stretched himself out on the child, and the flesh of the child became warm. He returned and walked back and forth in the house, and again went up and stretched himself out on him; then the child sneezed seven times, and the child opened his eyes (2 Kings 4:34-35).*

To me these verses depict a powerful account of the intercessory warfare of Elisha over this child. I can only imagine his prayer as he walked back and forth in the house. Some of my most intimate times with God were experienced as I walked back and forth in the house. I could share some testimonies of God's amazing presence and revelation knowledge that He imparted to me in times that I walked back and forth in the house as I prayed in His presence, with a passionate petition in pursuit of Him. My heart is rejoicing now as I reflect on some of those times of prayer.

It's interesting to me the way Elisha prayed. He literally covered the child with himself. How that depicts God's desire to cover every part of us! He wants nothing in us hurting or broken. He doesn't want to just repair portions of us.

The same applies to His church of which we are a part. Every part of the church is significant. Every ministry ordained of God in the church is important. All if it must be functioning properly, led by His Spirit, to be fully accomplishing successfully God's purpose.

In order for the church to be whole and complete, we must be constantly overshadowed by His presence and operating in His love.

> *Rather, let our lives lovingly express truth [in all things, speaking truly, dealing truly, living truly]. Enfolded in love, let us grow up in every way and in all things into Him Who is the Head, [even] Christ (the Messiah, the Anointed One). For because of Him the whole body (the church, in all its various parts), closely joined and firmly knit together by the joints and ligaments with which it is supplied, when each part [with power adapted to its need] is working properly [in all its functions], grows to full maturity, building itself up in love (Eph. 4:15-16 AMP).*

I can only imagine the joy Elisha felt when the child awakened. No doubt he could hardly contain his excitement. He knew and loved this family well. He had known this child since birth.

He immediately sent Gehazi to bring in the Shunammite woman. I imagine he was so anxious to see her receive her miracle. She had passionately petitioned God for this moment, and now her answer awaited her embrace.

> *And he called Gehazi and said, "Call this Shunammite woman." So he called her. And when she came in to him, he said, "Pick up your son." So she went in, fell at his feet, and bowed to the ground; then she picked up her son and went out (2 Kings 4:36-37).*

As much as any part of this story, verse 37 amazes me. She had experienced such a traumatic turn of events this day. Her entire life changed in a moment. She had held her son—her promise—as he died in her arms. She had deliberately taken him and placed him on the bed of the prophet and shut the door. Then she set out on a mission. She had proclaimed in faith that all would be well. She had pursued the presence of God and petitioned Him passionately at the feet of Elisha. She persuaded him to come back to her house. And then she had waited as Elisha had gone in to pray and now—now the door was opened to her and she was called in to her son. He was alive and well! All of her hopes and dreams were restored and alive again. Her beloved son was waiting for her loving embrace and she was so eager to hold him and hug him again. But, she came in where they were and first fell at Elisha's feet and worshiped God for her miracle. What a powerful moment we read in this verse. What a genuine heart of worship this mother demonstrated. She offered praise first and then picked up her son. No doubt, her praise was powerful and pure in the eyes of God and it was received and rewarded by Him.

Wouldn't you have loved to have seen her when she picked up her son, healed and whole!

Let us never forget from where the answers in answered prayers come. Let us never forget the Provider of the promise. Always remember to thank the Giver of good things. For He is worthy! By and through Him alone are all things possible.

> ### *I will make my praise powerful because my God is worthy and my heart is grateful!*

Read this passage from Psalm 103 carefully. Take in every word and meditate on it.

> *Bless (affectionately, gratefully praise) the Lord, O my soul; and all that is [deepest] within me, bless His holy name! Bless (affectionately, gratefully praise) the Lord, O my soul, and forget not [one of] all His benefits—Who forgives [every one of] all your iniquities, Who heals [each one of] all your diseases, Who redeems your life from the pit and corruption, Who beautifies, dignifies, and crowns you with loving-kindness and tender mercy; Who satisfies your mouth [your necessity and desire at your personal age and situation] with good so that your youth, renewed, is like the eagle's [strong, overcoming, soaring]! (Ps. 103:1-5 AMP)*

Take a moment and write your thoughts of gratitude based on the provisions and benefits that are mentioned in these five verses. What about this passage makes you realize how much God is worthy of our continual praise and gratitude?

_____

_____

_____

_____

_____

_____

_____

_____

_____

_____

God, give me a grateful heart. May I never forget Your many benefits. I pray that my praise will always be powerful, for You are so worthy to receive it.

As you journal and study this week, make a point to seek and study passages of praise. Make them a personal prayer and offer them as your praise to God.

What a wonderful example this loving wife and mother gave us to follow. She gave us insight on being a true warrior. She fought the gates of hell and won! We can do the same when we follow her example.

She made God's presence priority in her home and heart.
She made her proclamation positive based
on His Word and promises.
She made her pursuit proactive and was not
passive about God's guidance in her life.
She made her petition passionate as she prayed.
She made her praise powerful because
she recognized God was worthy of her gratitude.

I believe—even in the moments of her greatest pain—peace surfaced in her spirit. Her faith had taken hold and Satan lost his grip. She had to shut the door throughout the process of this entire battle. But I believe she kept her focus and supernatural peace prevailed throughout her dark times. She looked to where she was going and not where she was. Even though she had to walk out the valley, I believe she knew it would ultimately be temporary. And this produced peace—peace that passed understanding—even in the midst of the storm.

She experienced His perfect peace in the process of it all!

> *Then they cry out to the Lord in their trouble, And He brings them out of their distresses. He calms the storm, So that its waves are still. Then they are glad because they are quiet; So He guides them to their desired haven (Ps. 107:28-30).*

You may be in verse 28. But verse 29 follows and verse 30 is promised! Look beyond where you are to where you are going. His peace will be yours—even in the battle.

WEEK SIX
Prevailing Peace

In a Perilous World

"I will experience His perfect peace in the process of it all!"

In our final lesson this week, we will discuss that perfect peace that prevails even in the battles. We will talk about how to shut the door to fear and keep it shut. Peace is defined as a mental or spiritual condition marked by freedom from disquieting or oppressive thoughts or emotions; calmness of mind and heart; freedom from confusion.

In this world in which we live, we are bombarded with news that is disquieting and oppressive; upsetting thoughts and emotions are all around us; anxiety seems to be the norm; and anger and rage are commonplace reactions in public and private places alike. People are confused. Wrong is portrayed as right and evil is called good. Our politicians argue. The

> *No matter what the conflict we are in, emotions always play a role.*

daily news brings distressful information at a fast pace. Wars are raging between nations and neighbors. Reality TV is often nothing more than a mangled mess of people's personal sagas that the viewers invite into their living rooms and call entertainment. Social media has become an outlet for many to share their trouble and disdain of "friends" and family members. When you read it you get caught up in their battles. Peace is often only a fantasy in the minds of people around us. *But it shouldn't be so in the life of a believer.*

I often say that we have a cunning enemy who uses current events to give us careless emotions. He brings to us in numerous ways all sorts of distressing information about events going on around us. When we receive the distressing information in our hearts it brings fear, anxiety, and the absence of peace. *We replace the gift of His peace with the fear of the moment.*

Once we open the door to fear, all sorts of emotions flood in. Fear never comes in alone. It always travels with anxiety. Anxiety and anger are close friends. One always encourages the other to come to the party in your mind. And when anger has access to your thoughts, everything changes.

Emotions are fleeting and we should never make a decision guided by them. Emotions are the shallowest part of who we are. They come and go—sometimes quickly. So, we should guard our actions and words, as we have already discussed, especially when we are feeling emotional. We should never make a decision influenced by emotions alone.

There is a very interesting passage of Scripture that I want us to read and ponder. It is found in Genesis 4:6-7.

> *And the Lord said to Cain, Why are you angry? And why do you look sad and depressed and dejected? If you do well, will you not be accepted? And if you do not do*

well, sin crouches at your door; its desire is for you, but you must master it (AMP).

In this passage, God is addressing Cain and his downcast demeanor. Cain and his brother Abel had each prepared an offering for the Lord. God accepted Abel's offering but not Cain's (Genesis 4:3-5). The Lord is asking Cain why he is angry and explains to him that it's written all over his face.

God asks a question and provides the answer at the same time. He instructs Cain that if he does right, he will be accepted—no need to be angry, Cain, just do the right thing! But God warns Cain that if he doesn't, sin crouches at his door. He warns Cain that if he makes decisions in anger, it will cause him to open the door to sin. Sin was waiting just outside, desiring to master him. But God warns Cain that he must master it. This means that Cain could have mastered sin if he would have chosen to.

Look again at verse 6. Anger brought with it sadness, depression, and a dejected state of mind. Bad emotions travel in packs, and they come to devour peace.

We must heed this same warning. We must shut the door to sin that lurks outside when we are in an emotional state of mind. Marriages split up when people open the door during an emotional battle.

> ***Don't allow yourself to get caught up in careless emotions that cause you to open the door to the sin that crouches just outside.***

Closest friendships are lost when emotions run rampant and the door is opened before the emotional battle is settled. Business partners split up. Churches divide. It happens often all because someone opens the door to the pack of emotions led by anger. Open the door when angry, and sin runs in and brings destruction with it. Anger and its emotional companions shove peace right out.

Sadly, the very next verse we read gives us the choice Cain made and the results that followed.

> *And Cain said to his brother, Let us go out to the field.*
> *And when they were in the field, Cain rose up against*
> *Abel his brother and killed him (Gen. 4:8 AMP).*

Cain had just been in the presence of God. He had heard His voice and His clear warning and he completely and willfully disregarded it. And as a result, sin mastered him—all in a moment because of an emotional choice. Peace was now absent in Cain's life, and immediate and lasting regret set in. What a sad story.

I shared this passage with you to help illustrate how important it is that we shut the door to the sin that lurks just outside when we are in a battle. No matter what the conflict we are in, emotions always play a role. Your emotional weakness may not be anger. It may be something completely different. But remember, emotions travel in packs. It may be fear of the unknown. It could be stress from a battle that has lasted long. It could be condemnation (which often births self-disdain) from choices you've made. It could be regret, despair, dread, discouragement…the list goes on and on. All of these override peace.

The sin, sorrow, sickness, and situations that we all deal with from time to time—whether our own or someone's we love—bring emotions to the surface. If we do not deal with them, sin is waiting outside our door.

How do I keep that door shut? God told Cain to do well, and that if he did not do well sin was crouching, waiting to master him. Cain was angry at Abel. But it wasn't Abel's fault that God accepted his offering and not Cain's. Cain became angry and then jealous and vented his wrath in the direction of Abel. Instead of correcting himself and providing a proper offering, he took his anger and ran with it.

Remember God told Cain that he could master it. So then can we! We must recognize that the enemy is gifted at sneaking in through emotions. He especially loves anger. Anger, when left to itself, always causes problems. Remember, emotions always bring other emotions with them. Anger's companions can be especially nasty.

Let's look at some powerful instructions in the Word dealing with emotions that will help us to do well and make the right choices in times of emotional conflict.

> *When angry, do not sin; do not ever let your wrath (your exasperation, your fury or indignation) last until the sun goes down. Leave no [such] room or foothold for the devil [give no opportunity to him] (Eph. 4:26-27 AMP).*

> *Be angry [or stand in awe] and sin not; commune with your own hearts upon your beds and be silent (sorry for the things you say in your hearts). Selah [pause, and calmly think of that]! (Ps. 4:4 AMP)*

Both of these passages imply that there are certainly occasions when anger is the understood and accepted emotion. When you witness an injustice or experience unfair treatment, justified anger in and of itself it not a sin. However, reacting in the flesh while angry can result in sin. And brooding and harboring that anger is sin.

Read and meditate on these verses and honestly evaluate your own handling of anger.

> *Cease from anger and forsake wrath; fret not yourself— it tends only to evildoing. For evildoers shall be cut off,*

but those who wait and hope and look for the Lord [in the end] shall inherit the earth (Ps. 37:8-9 AMP).

He who is slow to anger has great understanding, but he who is hasty of spirit exposes and exalts his folly (Prov. 14:29 AMP).

Understand [this], my beloved brethren. Let every man be quick to hear [a ready listener], slow to speak, slow to take offense and to get angry. For man's anger does not promote the righteousness God [wishes and requires]. So get rid of all uncleanness and the rampant outgrowth of wickedness, and in a humble (gentle, modest) spirit receive and welcome the Word which implanted and rooted [in your hearts] contains the power to save your souls. But be doers of the Word [obey the message], and not merely listeners to it, betraying yourselves [into deception by reasoning contrary to the Truth] (James 1:19-22 AMP).

But now put away and rid yourselves [completely] of all these things: anger, rage, bad feeling toward others, curses and slander, and foulmouthed abuse and shameful utterances from your lips! (Col. 3:8 AMP)

These verses may sound harsh if you are struggling with anger issues. But remember, anger always robs you of peace and never comes in alone. God will help you and you can rid yourself of anger and <u>shut the door</u> to the emotions that come with it. <u>Sin may be crouching at the door, but it cannot come in if you keep it shut.</u>

I am not a professional counselor, but I do minister one on one at times with the Word of God as my guide for hurting people. I have met a lot of people in this life who were troubled emotionally and anger was the root. I have prayed with them and for them in their struggles. I, too, have experienced my own times when I let anger get the best of me.

Like in Cain's story, anger brought with it sadness, depression, and a dejected spirit. And like Cain, it showed on their countenance. God wants His people set free from these unhealthy emotions. His Word and His power can do just that!

Take a moment and sincerely pray and ask God to allow His Spirit to minister to you and free you of emotions that are displeasing to Him.
Pray that His peace will replace the pain that is caused in your heart by unhealthy emotions.

How do we <u>shut the door</u> to unhealthy emotions? Or like Cain was instructed, how do we keep it shut and master that sin that waits to master us?

Let's read this beloved verse and think on what Jesus was saying to us.

> *Peace I leave with you, My peace I give to you; not as the world gives do I give to you. Let not your heart be troubled, neither let it be afraid (John 14:27).*

Jesus was preparing His disciples for His soon departure. They didn't understand all He was trying to prepare them for and He wanted them to know that He would not leave them without a Comforter (see John 14:16-18). He also told them that He would leave them peace—His perfect peace—to abide in. He has done the same for us! It is a gift from Jesus, our Prince of Peace and Peace Speaker.

I also love this verse that Jesus spoke while continuing to address those closest to Him as He prepared them for what was about to come. He would soon be crucified and everything in their world would change forever. They couldn't grasp it at the moment, but these would be cherished words that they would hold to and understand later.

> *These things I have spoken to you, that in Me you may have peace. In the world you will have tribulation; but be of good cheer, I have overcome the world (John 16:33).*

Just a few months ago, I read this beloved verse in John differently than I had ever read it before. Jesus ended His words of comfort with this verse just before going to pray that beautiful prayer of intercession recorded in John 17.

He spoke this powerful statement to His disciples saying, "be of good cheer, I have overcome the world," *before* He ever went to the garden to pray; *before* He was so pressed that His sweat became drops of blood; *before* He felt the brutal beating on His back or the cruel crown of thorns placed on His head; *before* the pain of Calvary's nails. He was looking past where He was—fully aware of what He was facing—focusing instead on where He was going. His focus—His perspective—was beyond the moment. He knew He had His greatest valley just before Him, but *He shut the door* to His own emotions and saw His greatest victory. And His greatest victory became ours.

No matter the valley before us, as we addressed in the first week of our study, if we have proper perspective it changes everything. It will enable you to shut the door to unhealthy emotions when you remember the struggle is temporary but His promises are eternal.

Jesus declared before His triumphant victory over death, hell, and the grave that He had already overcome the world. Through faith in Him and by His power, so have we!

✳   Don't allow yourself to get caught up in careless emotions that cause you to open the door to the sin that crouches just outside. Look past the anger, the hurt, the fear. Look past the moment and see in faith your coming victory. Master the sin at hand by taking the hand of the Master. You are an overcomer. Victory is yours!

"Now" is a word we love. We don't like to wait. Once you have looked past where you are to where you are going by faith, you can experience the "now" of His peace.

> *Now may the God of hope fill you with all joy and peace in believing, that you may abound in hope by the power of the Holy Spirit (Rom. 15:13).*

Hallelujah for the God of Hope! He fills us with all joy and peace by the power of the Holy Spirit.

That same sweet Holy Spirit enables you to bear fruit that is in stark contrast to the emotions that drive out peace. The fruit of the Spirit abiding in you enables you to properly process your emotions. He enables you to stand against the fleshly tendencies that cause sin to master you.

> *But the fruit of the Spirit is love, joy, peace, longsuffering, kindness, goodness, faithfulness, gentleness, self-control. Against such there is no law. And those who are Christ's have crucified the flesh with its passions and desires. If we live in the Spirit, let us also walk in the Spirit. Let us not become conceited, provoking one another, envying one another (Gal. 5:22-26).*

Ask God to let the fruit of His Spirit increase in your life. Search your heart. Honestly evaluate the areas where you need growth and specifically request that the Lord lead you to produce more fruit in those areas. You will shut the door to the enemy more and more easily as the fruit of the Spirit increases in your walk with God.

Your thought process changes when the door is shut to improper emotions that rob your peace. You find yourself less stressed and less anxious. Read these familiar verses in Philippians again and ask God to help you apply them daily. Remember, we discussed in week four, that just declaring—positively proclaiming—the word alone isn't enough. We said that as powerful as our words are, words alone are not enough. As necessary as it is for us to speak the truth, we must also seek *the* Truth. Jesus is the Way and the Truth and the Life. Without a relationship with Him, our words, even if they are true, are hollow. We must know God and serve Him in order for His words and promises to be effective in our lives. Quoting the Word of God alone isn't enough. Picking favorite verses and claiming them as your own will not suffice without a relationship with Jesus. He is the Word made Flesh. To know Him and live for Him activates the power of His Word in us. Seek to know Him as never before, and the passages we are studying now will impact your life greatly as you speak and declare them over yourself.

> *Do not fret or have any anxiety about anything, but in every circumstance and in everything, by prayer and petition (definite requests), with thanksgiving, continue to make your wants known to God. And God's peace [shall be yours, that tranquil state of a soul assured of its salvation through Christ, and so fearing nothing from God and being content with its earthly lot of whatever sort that is, that peace] which transcends all understanding shall garrison and mount guard over your hearts and minds in Christ Jesus. For the rest, brethren, whatever is true, whatever is worthy of reverence and is honorable and seemly, whatever is just, whatever is pure, whatever is lovely and lovable,*

whatever is kind and winsome and gracious, if there is any virtue and excellence, if there is anything worthy of praise, think on and weigh and take account of these things [fix your minds on them] (Phil. 4:6-8 AMP).

And let the peace (soul harmony which comes) from Christ rule (act as umpire continually) in your hearts [deciding and settling with finality all questions that arise in your minds, in that peaceful state] to which as [members of Christ's] one body you were also called [to live]. And be thankful (appreciative), [giving praise to God always]. Let the word [spoken by] Christ (the Messiah) have its home [in your hearts and minds] and dwell in you in [all its] richness, as you teach and admonish and train one another in all insight and intelligence and wisdom [in spiritual things, and as you sing] psalms and hymns and spiritual songs, making melody to God with [His] grace in your hearts (Col. 3:15-16 AMP).

Write a sincere prayer asking that these verses come alive in your heart. Ask God to help you take the instructions given in these passages and practice them daily. Then the door to careless emotions will be shut in your heart.

_____

_____

_____

_____

_____

_____

_____

_____

_____

As we conclude this last lesson in our study, my earnest and heartfelt prayer is that you have learned how to effectively shut the door to the enemy and walk out your life in victory. We will have battles. Jesus said we would experience tribulation. But be courageous! He has already overcome for us.

Perilous times are here in this world, but not in my house. I will walk in His peace. I will shut the door to the enemy and I will be mindful of his strategy.

And I am determined that:

I will make God's presence priority
in my home and heart.
I will make my proclamation positive
based on His Word and promises.
I will make my pursuit proactive and will not be
passive about God's guidance in my life.
I will make my petition passionate and
I will pray as the Holy Spirit leads.
I will make my praise powerful because
my God is worthy and my heart is grateful.
And I will experience His perfect peace
in the process of it all.

Conclusion

Perhaps the most important door we will ever shut is the one Jesus talks about in this verse:

> *But you, when you pray, go into your room, and when you have shut your door, pray to your Father who is in the secret place; and your Father who sees in secret will reward you openly (Matt. 6:6).*

Jesus instructs us in this verse how important it is to spend time alone with Him.

Spending time privately with God will bring rewards in this life and in the life to come.

For us to walk in complete victory, we must spend quality time in communion with God. We must daily *Shut the Door* as instructed in this verse and separate ourselves for prayer. When we do,

We dismiss all distractions,
offer adoration,

> *pour out our petitions*
> *and lovingly listen*
> *for His reply.*

It's in our prayer closet, when we shut the door to all distractions, that He will lead, guide, and direct us in our journey in this life.

When we shut the door and spend quality time with God, we will be wise and know how to shut the door to the enemy and his tactics and keep it shut.

Shut the Door to the enemy and watch God open His door to your purpose.

And that door, no power can shut!

> *It's in our prayer closet, when we shut the door to all distractions, that He will lead, guide, and direct us in our journey in this life.*

"I know your works. See, I have set before you an open door, and no one can shut it; for you have a little strength, have kept My word, and have not denied My name (Rev. 3:8).

Shut the door to the enemy's plot and you will open the door to God's purpose for your life. And you will soon rejoice in the discovery that God's plans for you are better than your dreams!

About the Author

Rhonda K. Holland is a women's conference and retreat speaker, minister and teacher of the Word. She and her husband, Kenneth, have two adult sons, Joel and Jonathan. Rhonda is on staff at the South Aiken Church of God in South Carolina, where she and her family are involved in various areas of ministry. She has a passion and desire to minister to the body of Christ in these last days. Her heart for God and her love for the Word are felt as she ministers to those hurting and hungry for His presence.

Shut the Door